FOR ORGANS, PIANOS & ELECTRONIC KEYBOARDS

E-Z PLAY® TODAY

273

Christmas Time Is Here

MW01485087

ISBN 0-634-04744-2

7777 W. BLUEMOUND RD. P.O. BOX 13819 MILWAUKEE, WI 53213

E-Z PLAY® TODAY Music Notation © 1975 by HAL LEONARD CORPORATION

E-Z PLAY and EASY ELECTRONIC KEYBOARD MUSIC are registered trademarks of HAL LEONARD CORPORATION.

Visit Hal Leonard Online at
www.halleonard.com

CONTENTS

All Is Well

Registration 1
Rhythm: Waltz

Words and Music by Michael W. Smith
and Wayne Kirkpatrick

5

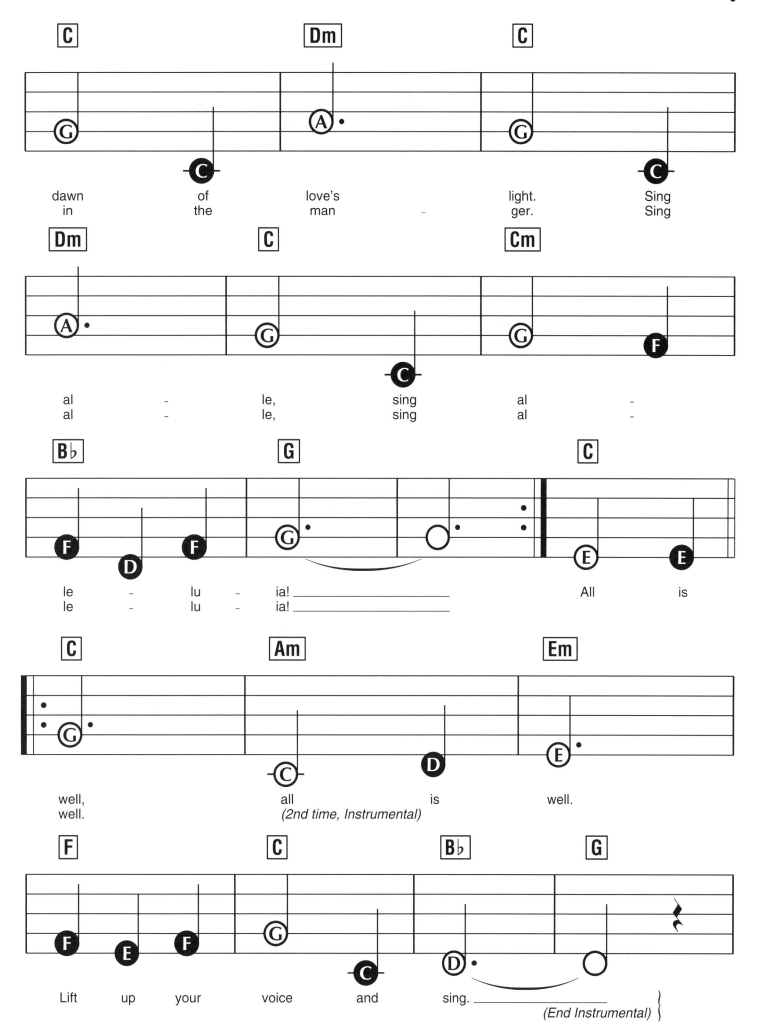

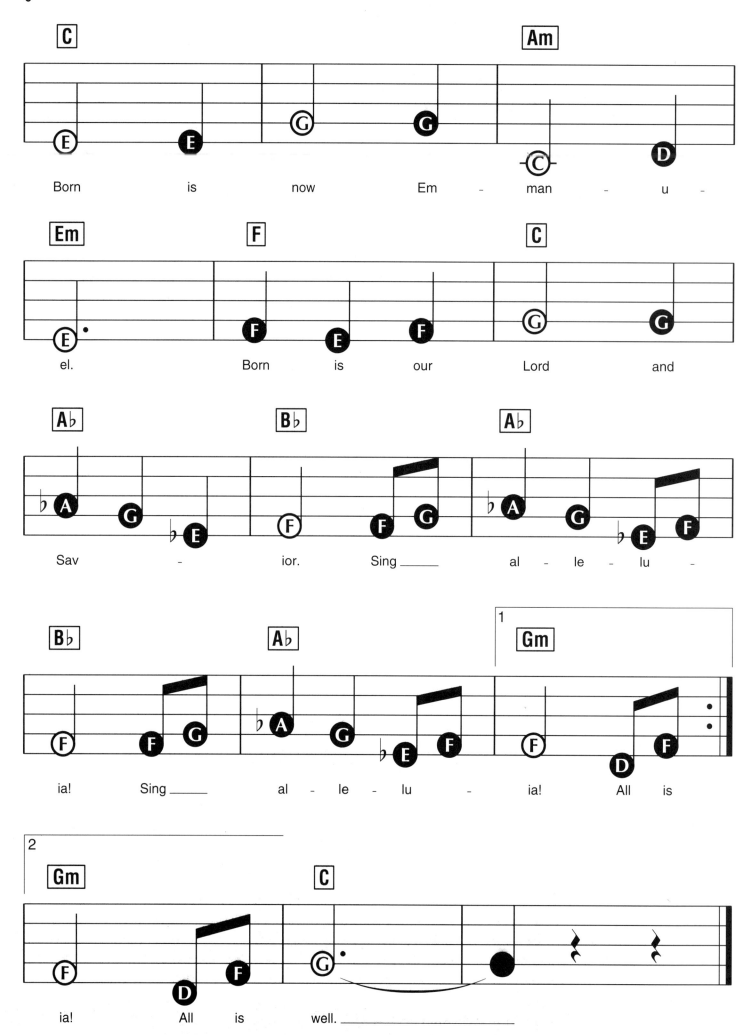

As Long as There's Christmas
from Walt Disney's
BEAUTY AND THE BEAST - THE ENCHANTED CHRISTMAS

Registration 3
Rhythm: Waltz

Music by Rachel Portman
Lyrics by Don Black

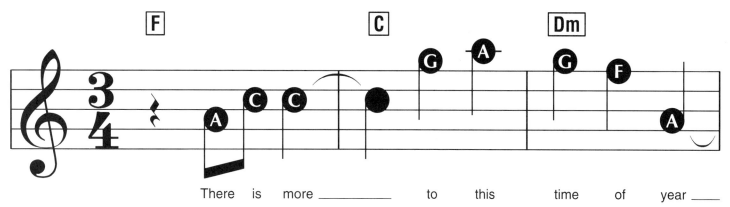

There is more _____ to this time of year _____

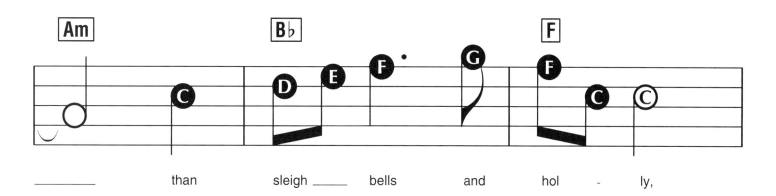

_____ than sleigh ____ bells and hol - ly,

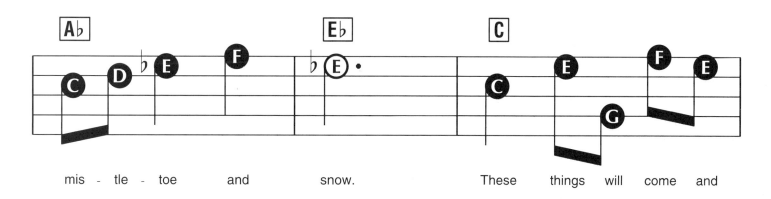

mis - tle - toe and snow. These things will come and

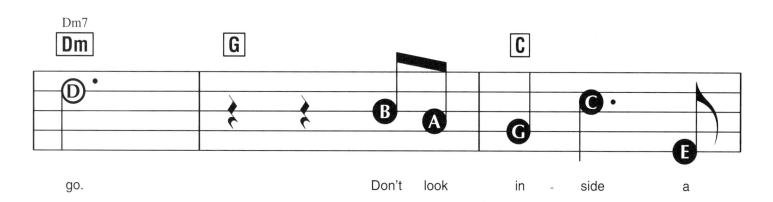

go. Don't look in - side a

8

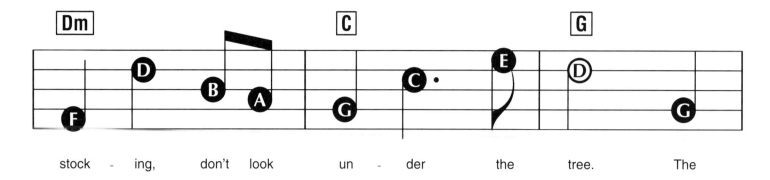

stock - ing, don't look un - der the tree. The

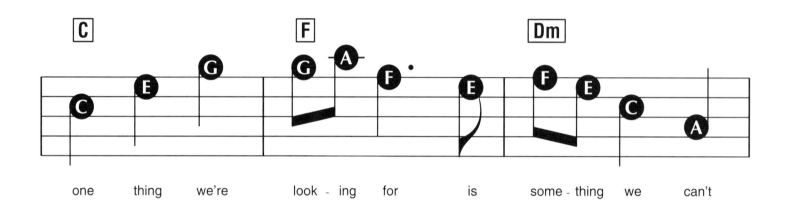

one thing we're look - ing for is some - thing we can't

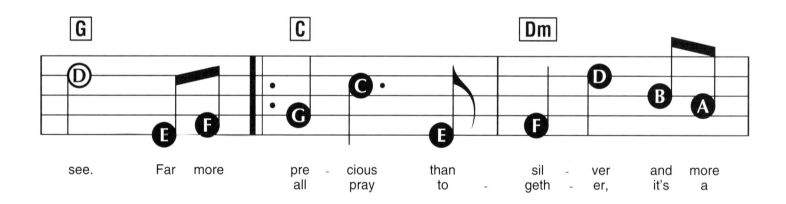

see. Far more pre - cious than sil - ver and more
all pray to - geth - er, it's a

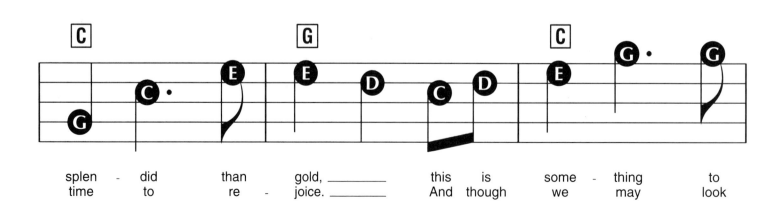

splen - did than gold, _____ this is some - thing to
time to re - joice. _____ And though we may look

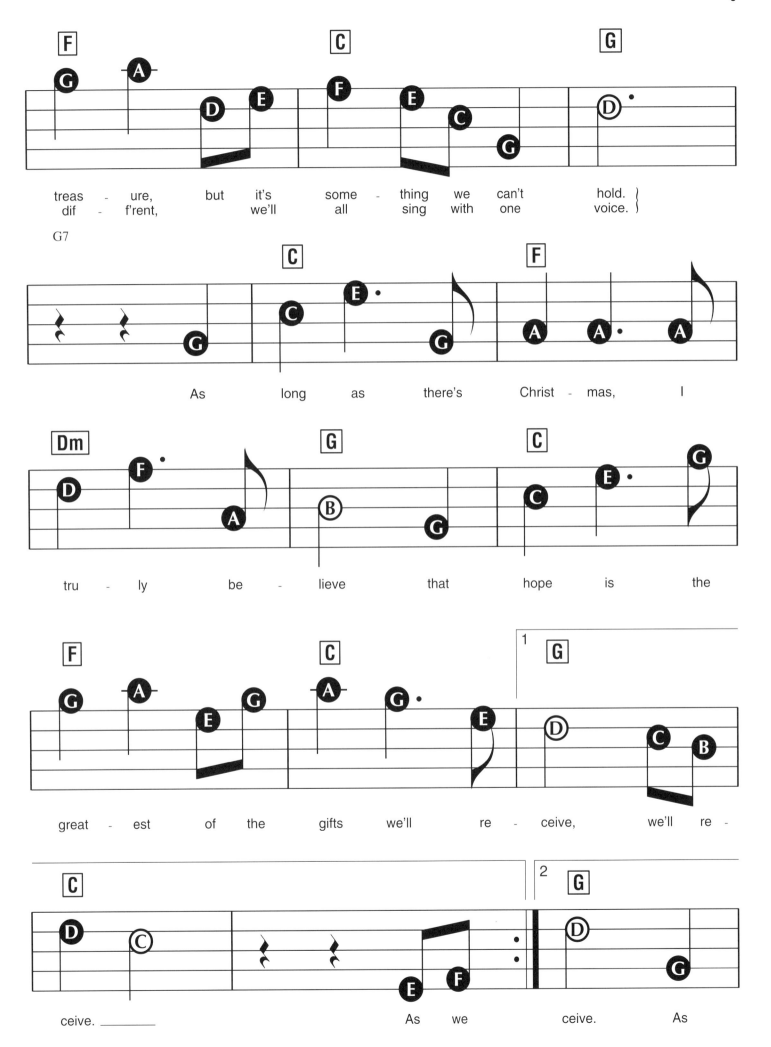

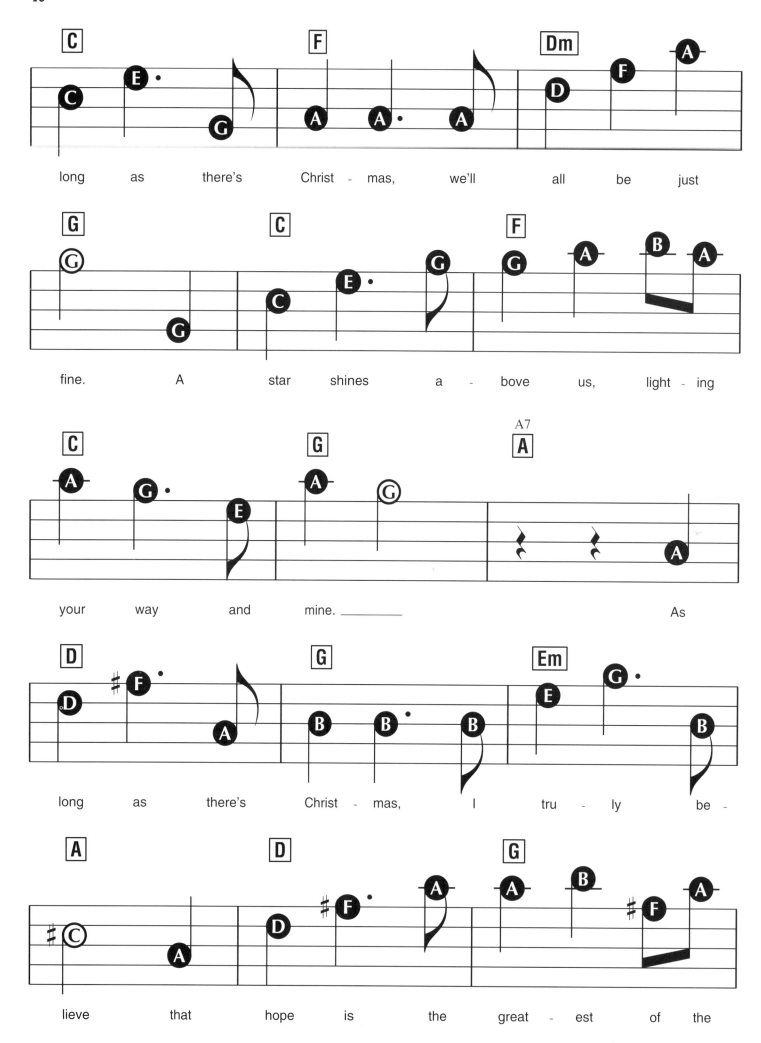

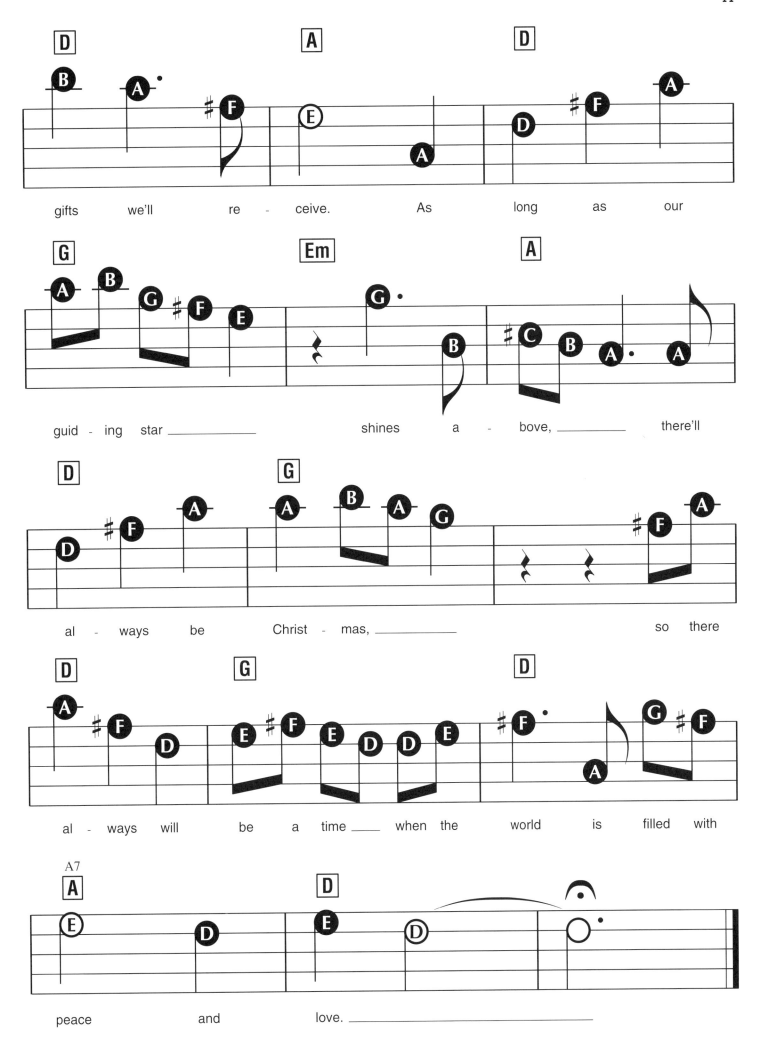

Because It's Christmas
(For All the Children)

Registration 2
Rhythm: Swing

Music by Barry Manilow
Lyric by Bruce Sussman and Jack Feldman

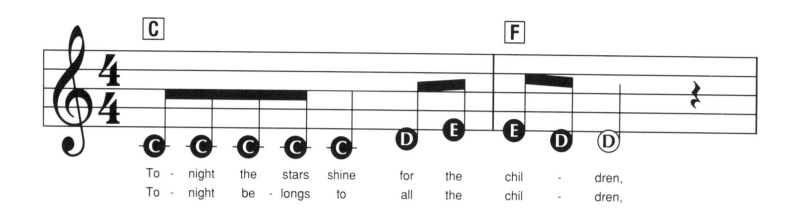

To - night the stars shine for the chil - dren,
To - night be - longs to all the chil - dren,

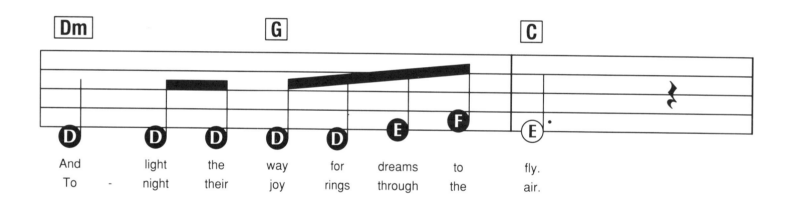

And light the way for dreams to fly.
To - night their joy for rings through the air.

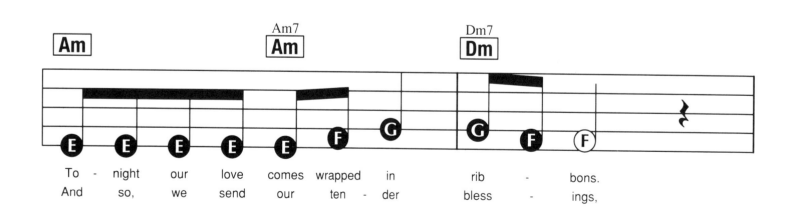

To - night our love comes wrapped in rib - bons.
And so, we send our ten - der bless - ings,

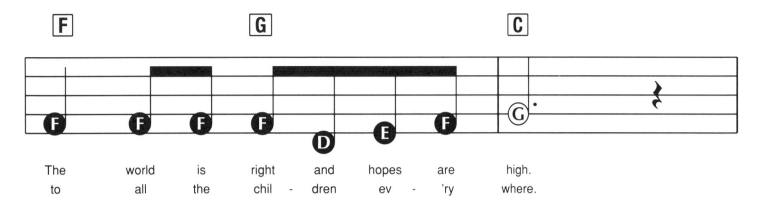

The world is right and hopes are high.
to all the right chil - dren ev - 'ry where.

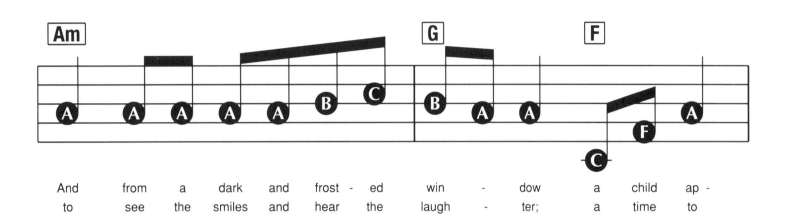

And from a dark and frost - ed win - dow a child ap -
to see the smiles and hear the laugh - ter; a time to

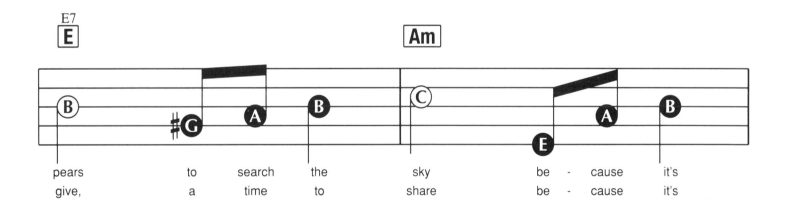

pears to search the sky be - cause it's
give, a time to share be - cause it's

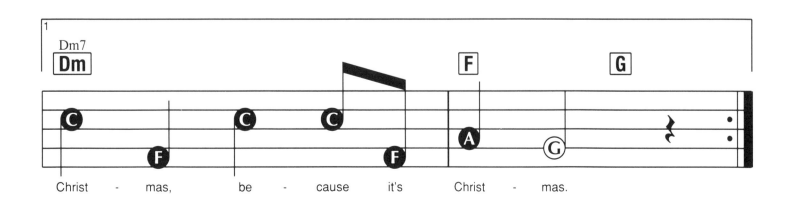

Christ - mas, be - cause it's Christ - mas.

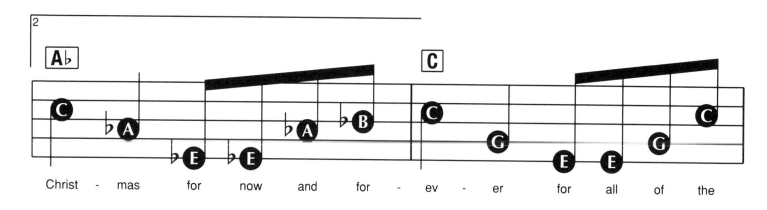

Christ - mas for now and for - ev - er for all of the

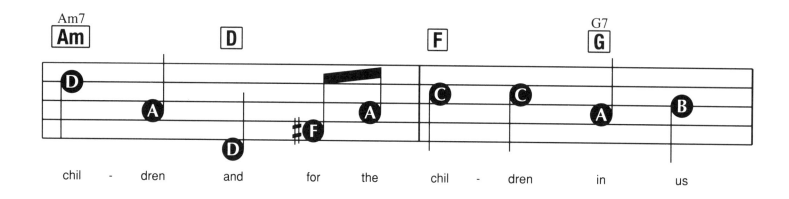

chil - dren and for the chil - dren in us

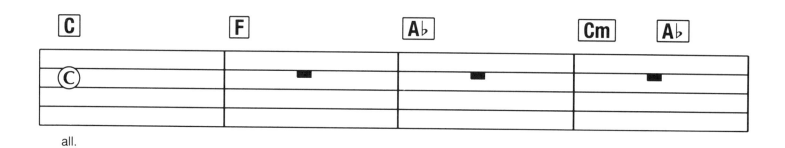

all.

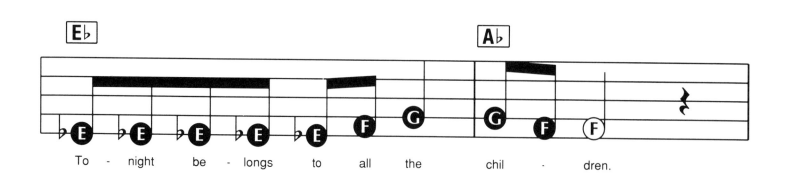

To - night be - longs to all the chil - dren.

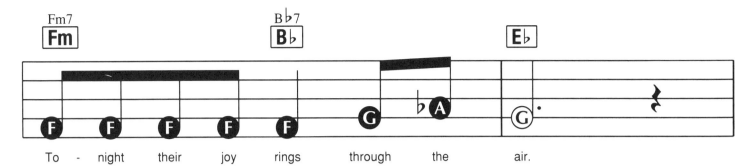

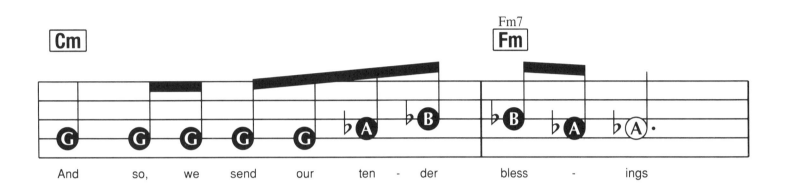

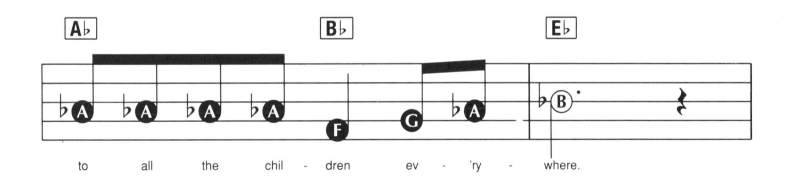

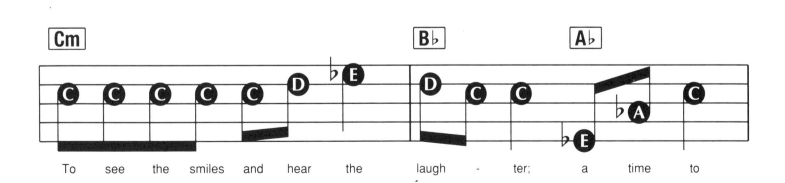

16

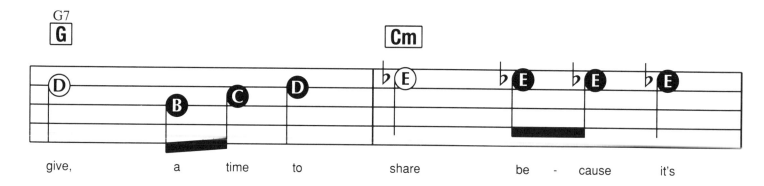

give, a time to share be - cause it's

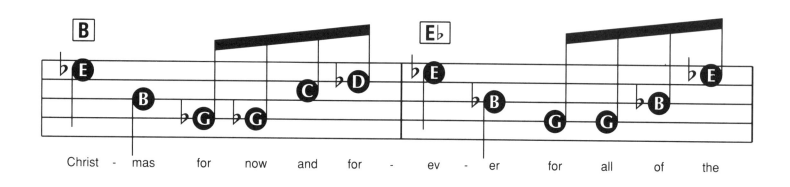

Christ - mas for now and for - ev - er for all of the

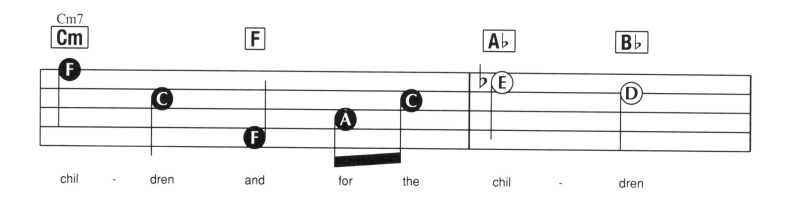

chil - dren and for the chil - dren

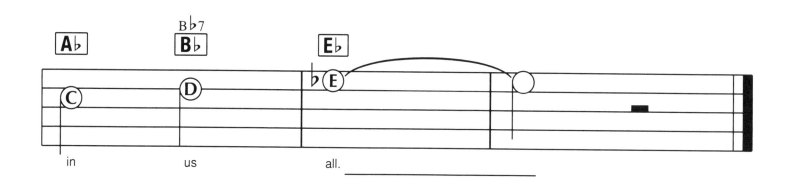

in us all.

The Bells of Christmas

Registration 1
Rhythm: Swing

Music by Barry Manilow
Lyrics by Adrienne Anderson

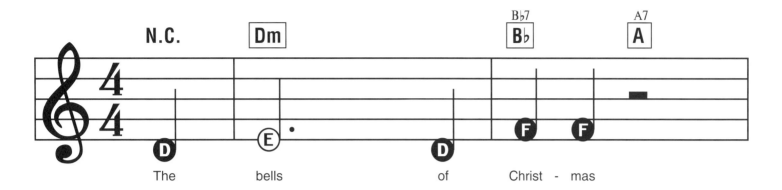

The bells of Christ - mas

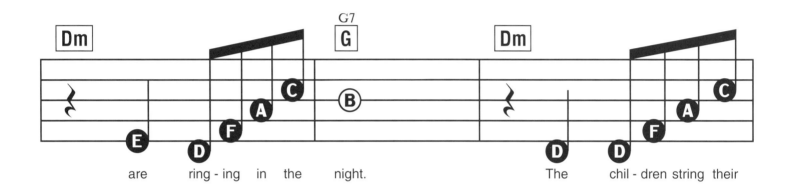

are ring - ing in the night. The chil - dren string their

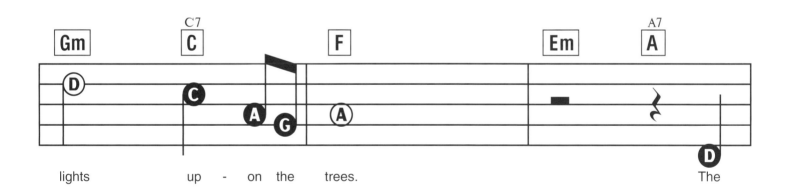

lights up - on the trees. The

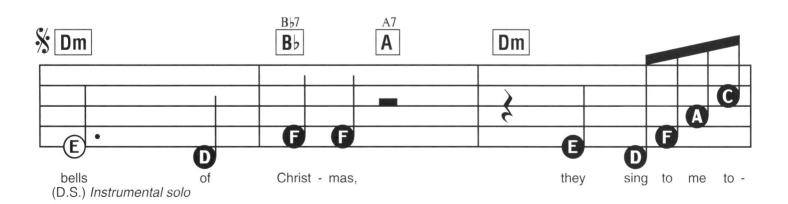

bells of Christ - mas, they sing to me to -
(D.S.) *Instrumental solo*

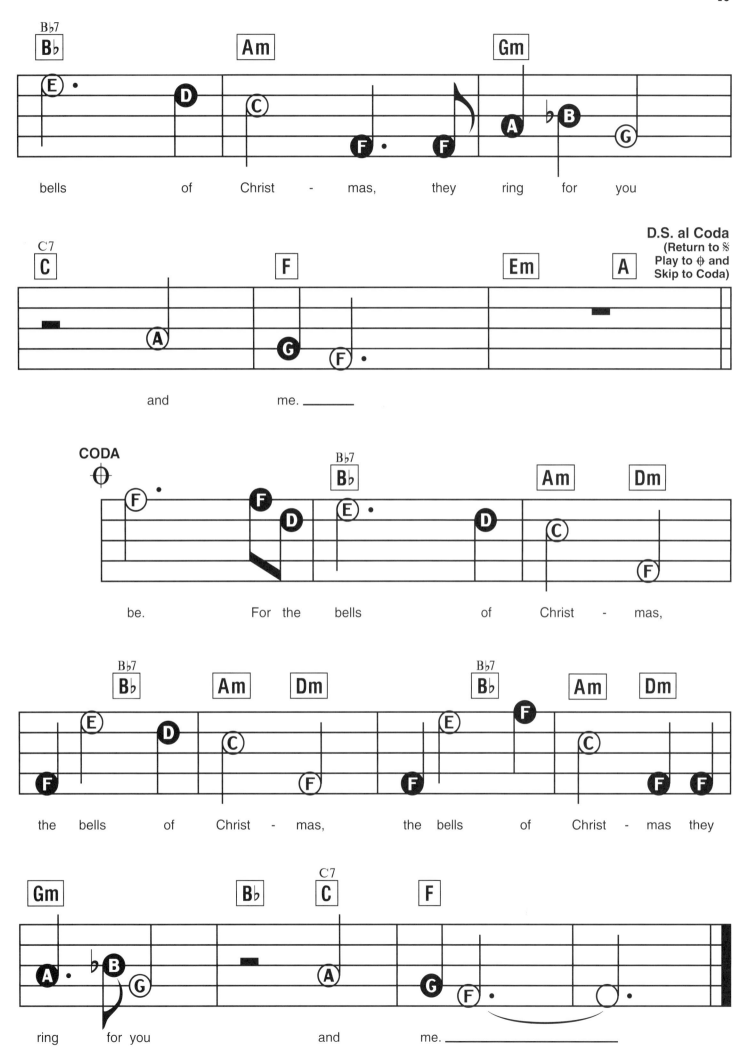

The Bells of St. Mary's

Registration 4
Rhythm: Fox Trot or Swing

Words by Douglas Furber
Music by A. Emmett Adams

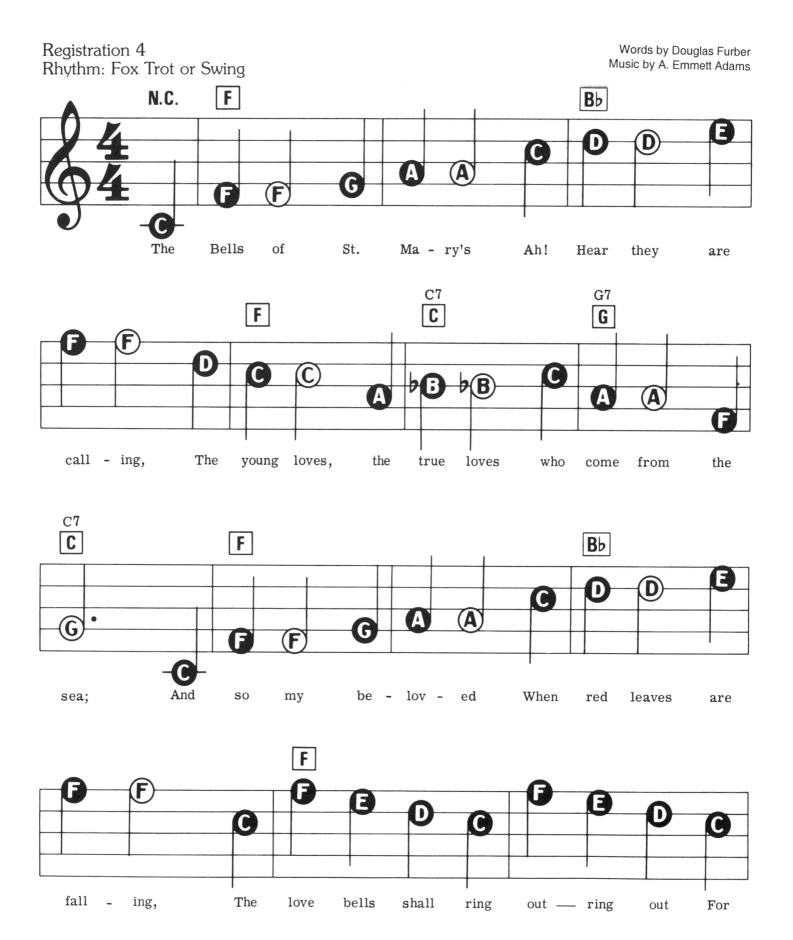

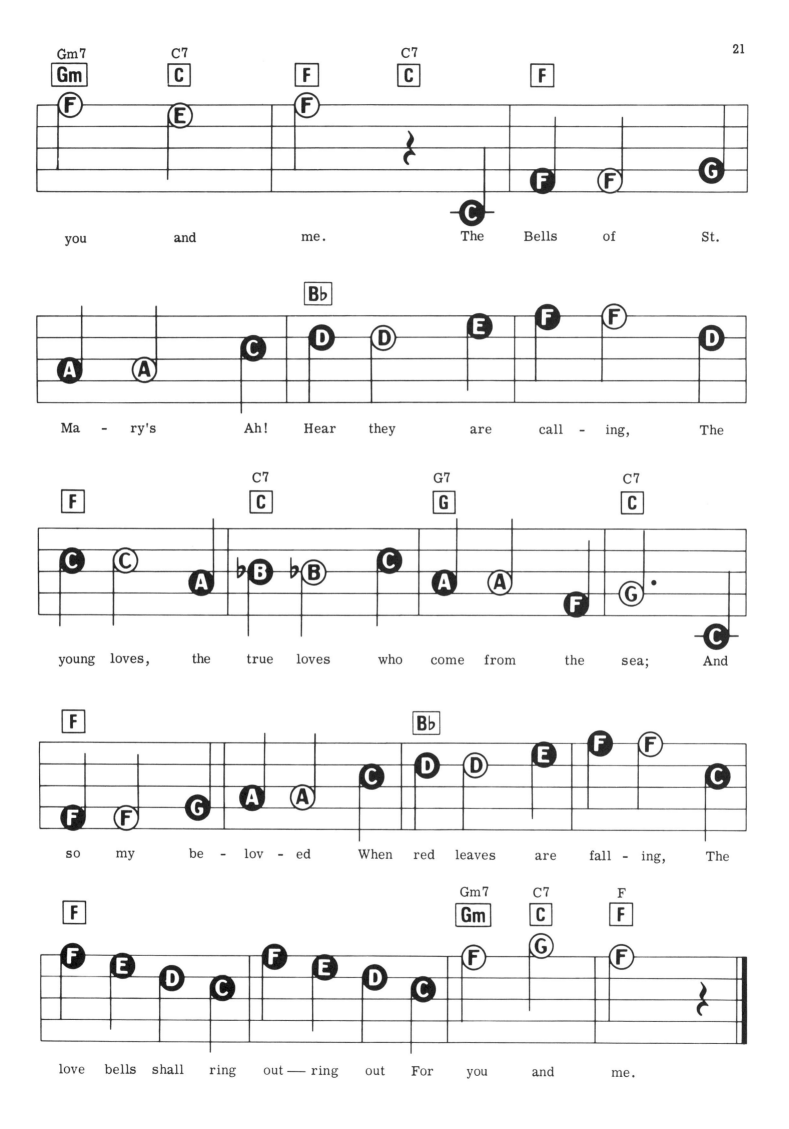

Caroling, Caroling

Registration 5
Rhythm: 6/8 March or Waltz

Words by Wihla Hutson
Music by Alfred Burt

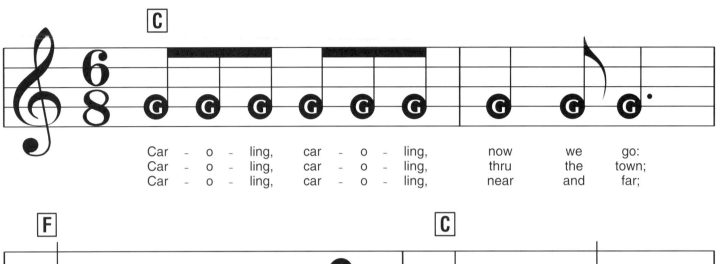

Car - o - ling, car - o - ling, now we go:
Car - o - ling, car - o - ling, thru the town;
Car - o - ling, car - o - ling, near and far;

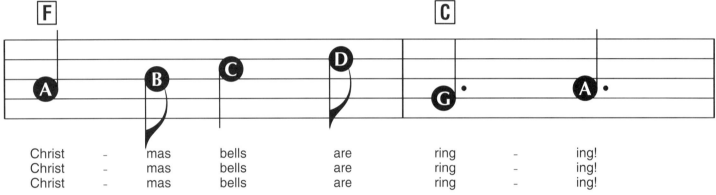

Christ - mas bells are ring - ing!
Christ - mas bells are ring - ing!
Christ - mas bells are ring - ing!

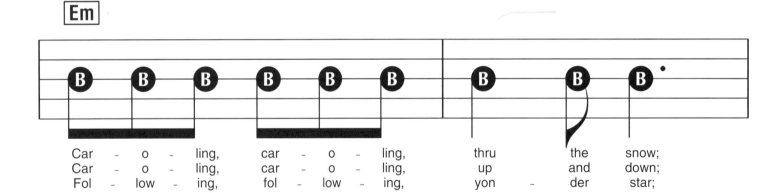

Car - o - ling, car - o - ling, thru the snow;
Car - o - ling, car - o - ling, up and down;
Fol - low - ing, fol - low - ing, yon - der star;

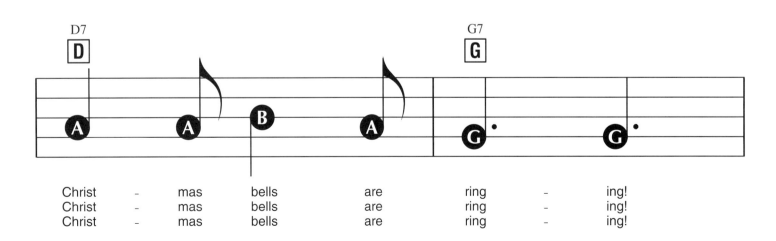

Christ - mas bells are ring - ing!
Christ - mas bells are ring - ing!
Christ - mas bells are ring - ing!

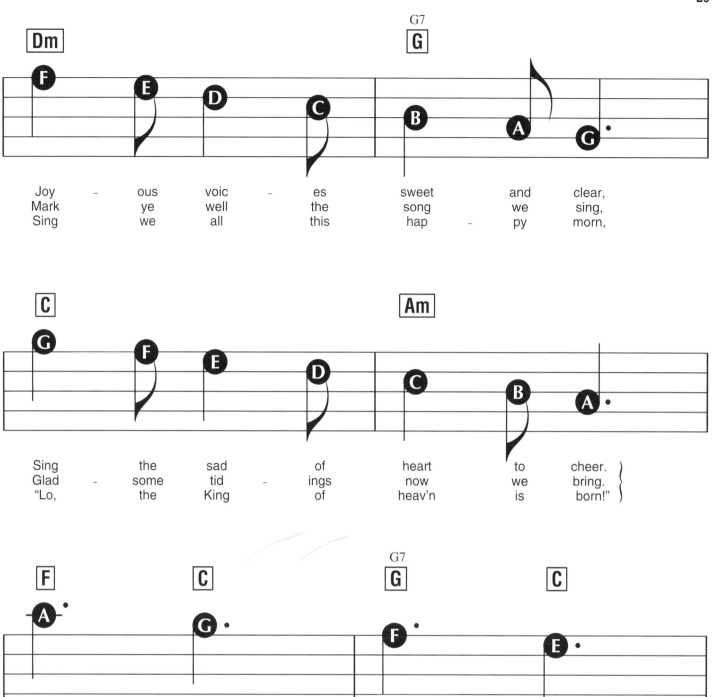

Joy - ous voic - es sweet and clear,
Mark ye well the song we sing,
Sing we all this hap - py morn,

Sing the sad of heart to cheer.
Glad - some the tid - ings now we bring.
"Lo, the King of heav'n is born!"

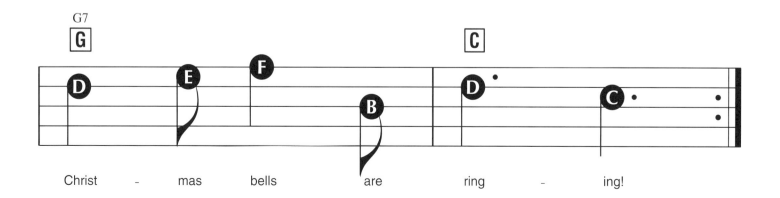

Ding, dong, ding, dong,

Christ - mas bells are ring - ing!

Celebrate the Child

Registration 2
Rhythm: 4/4 Ballad or 8 Beat

Words and Music by
Michael Card

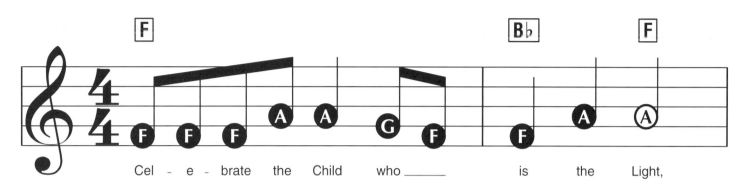

Cel - e - brate the Child who _____ is the Light,

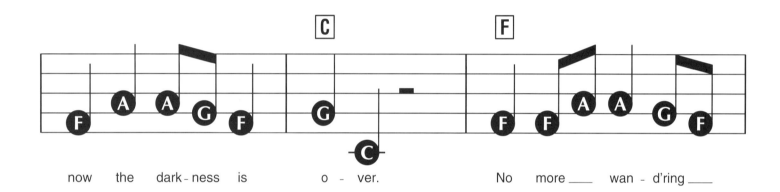

now the dark - ness is o - ver. No more ___ wan - d'ring ___

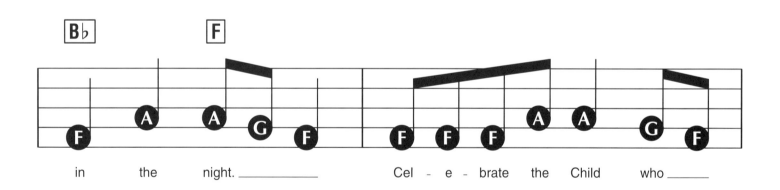

in the night. _____ Cel - e - brate the Child who _____

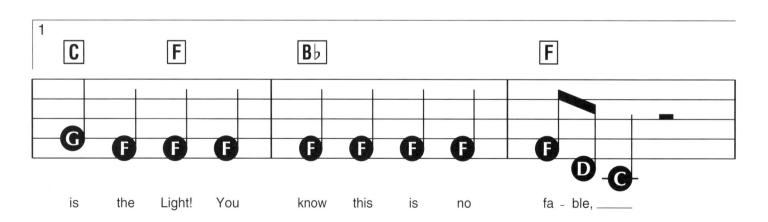

is the Light! You know this is no fa - ble, _____

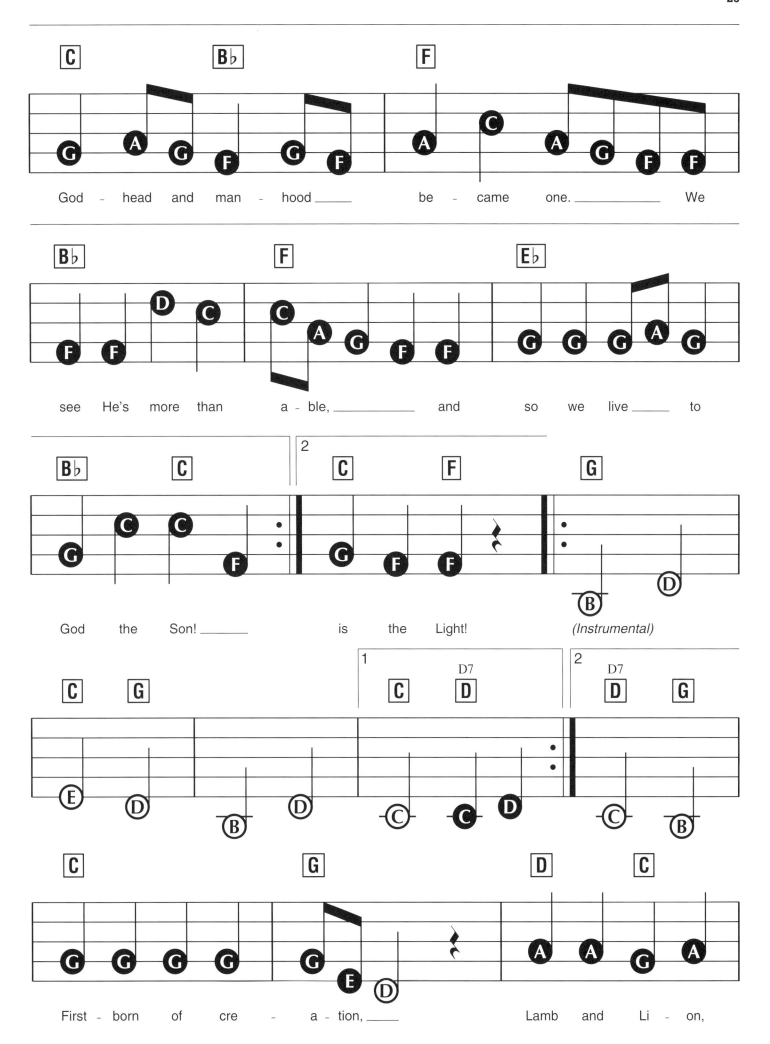

26

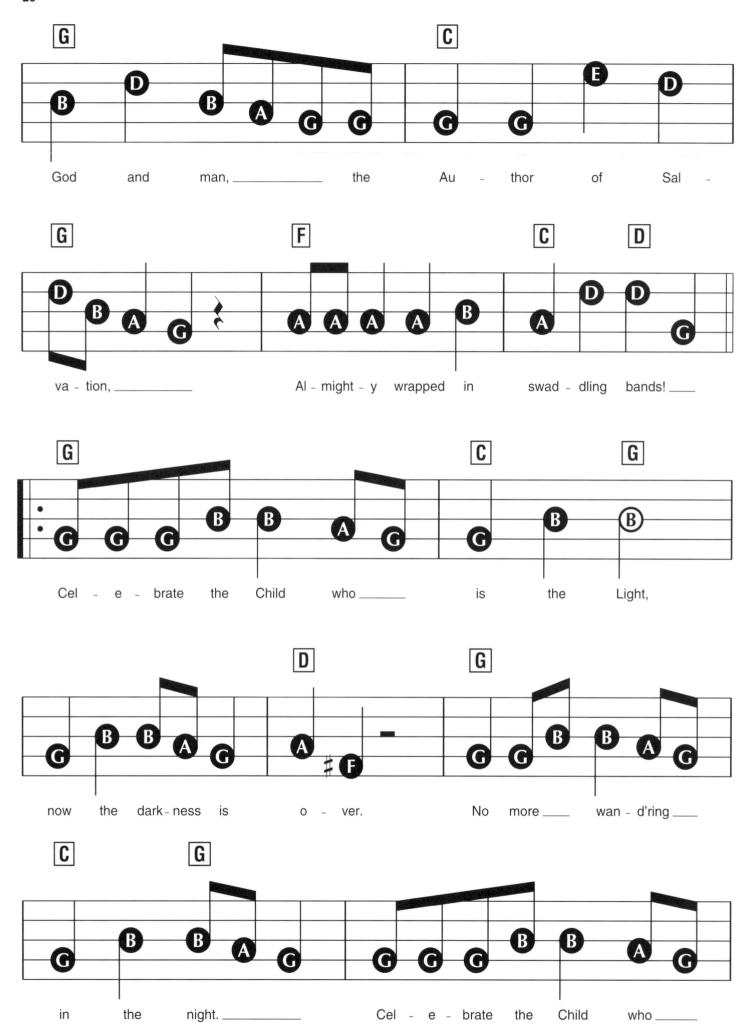

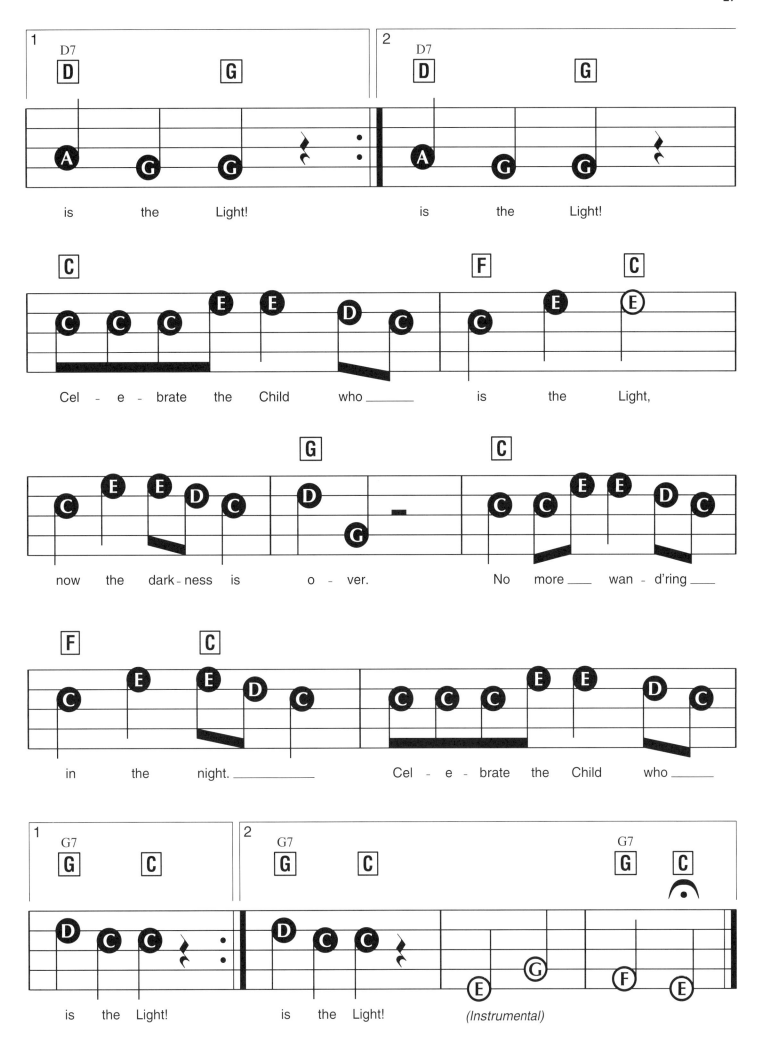

The Christmas Shoes

Registration 2
Rhythm: 4/4 Ballad or Fox Trot

Words and Music by Leonard Ahlstrom
and Eddie Carswell

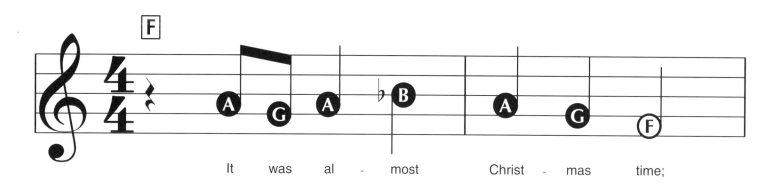

It was al - most Christ - mas time;

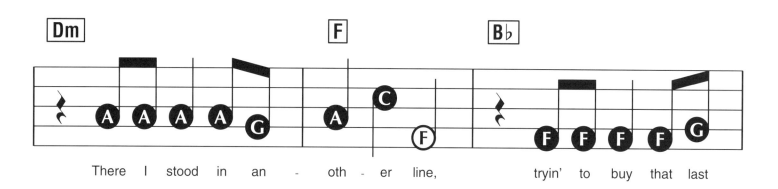

There I stood in an - oth - er line, tryin' to buy that last

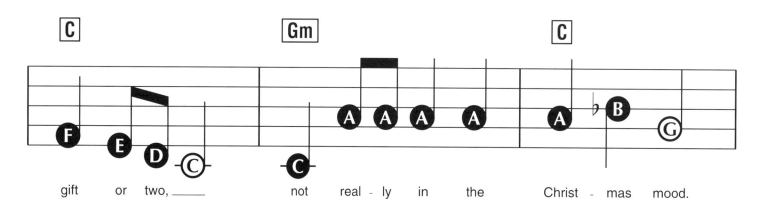

gift or two, _____ not real - ly in the Christ - mas mood.

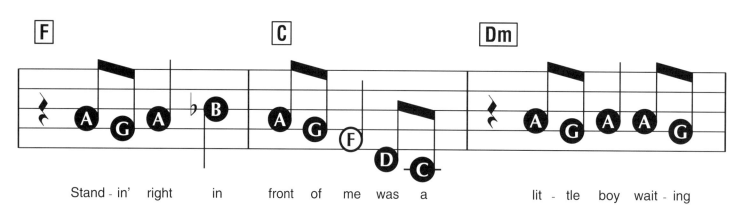

Stand - in' right in front of me was a lit - tle boy wait - ing

29

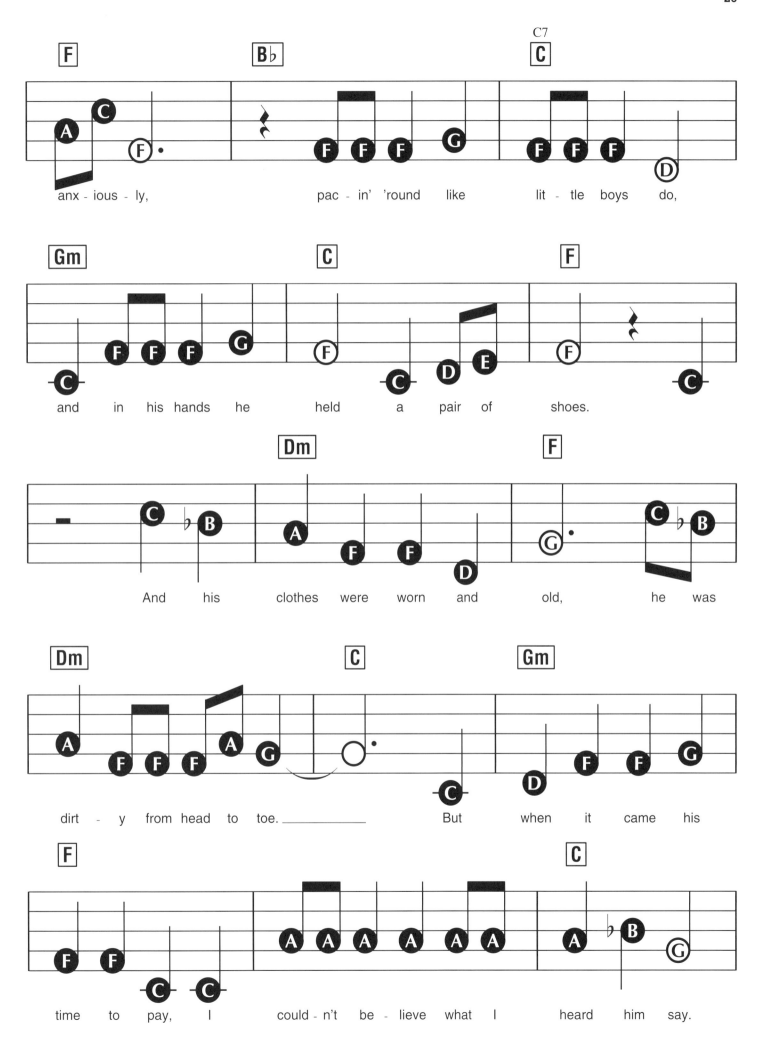

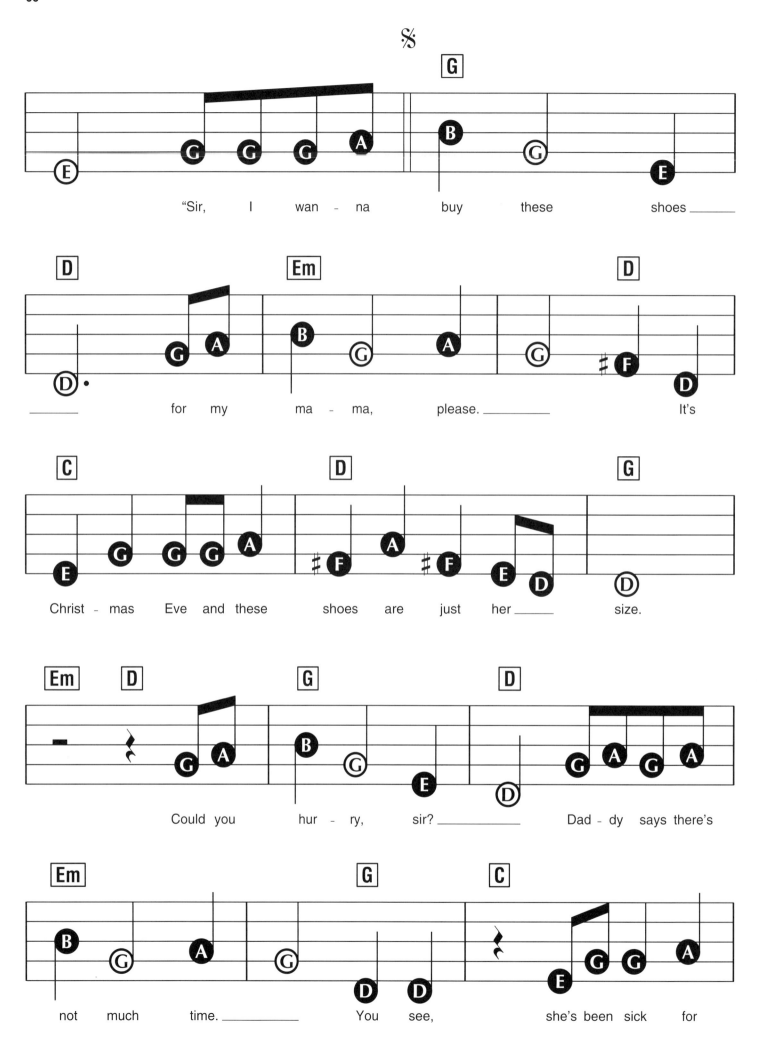

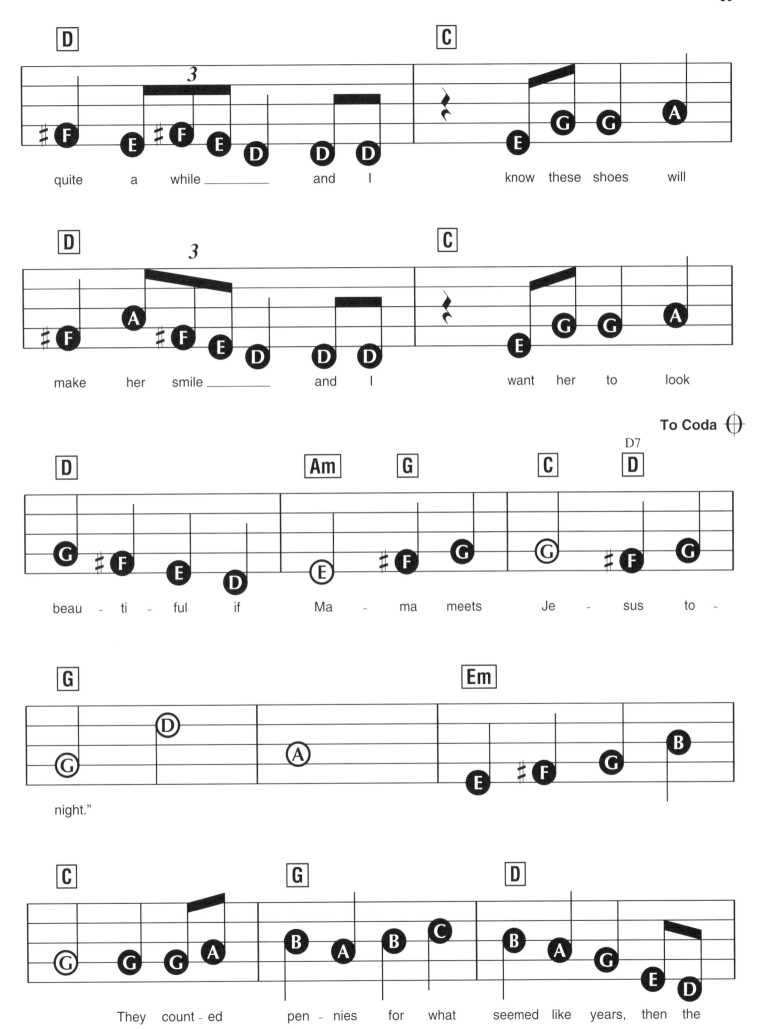

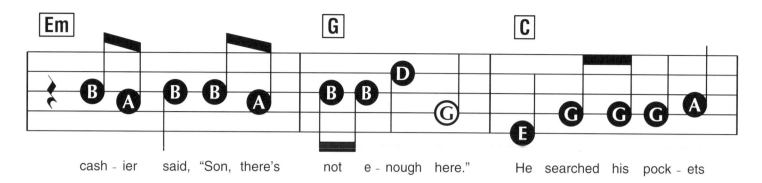

cash – ier said, "Son, there's not e – nough here." He searched his pock – ets

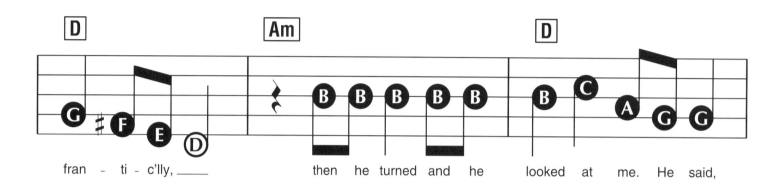

fran – ti – c'lly, _____ then he turned and he looked at me. He said,

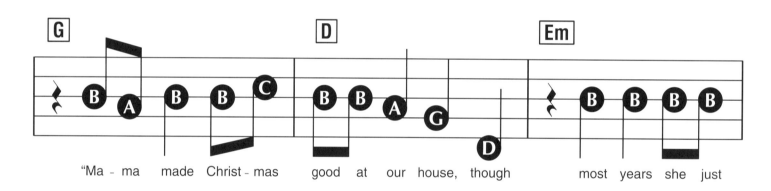

"Ma – ma made Christ – mas good at our house, though most years she just

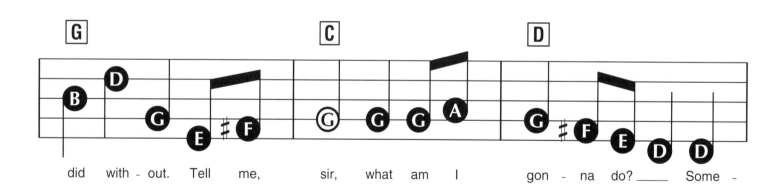

did with – out. Tell me, sir, what am I gon – na do? _____ Some –

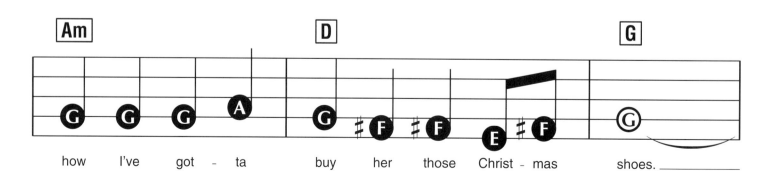

how I've got – ta buy her those Christ – mas shoes. _____

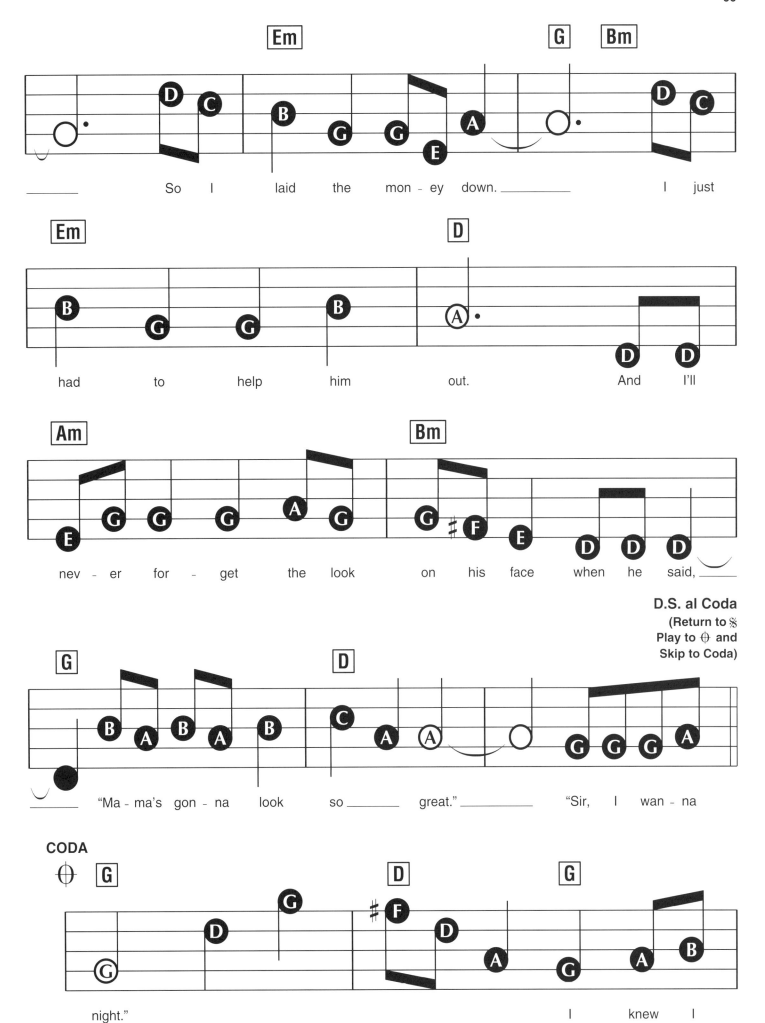

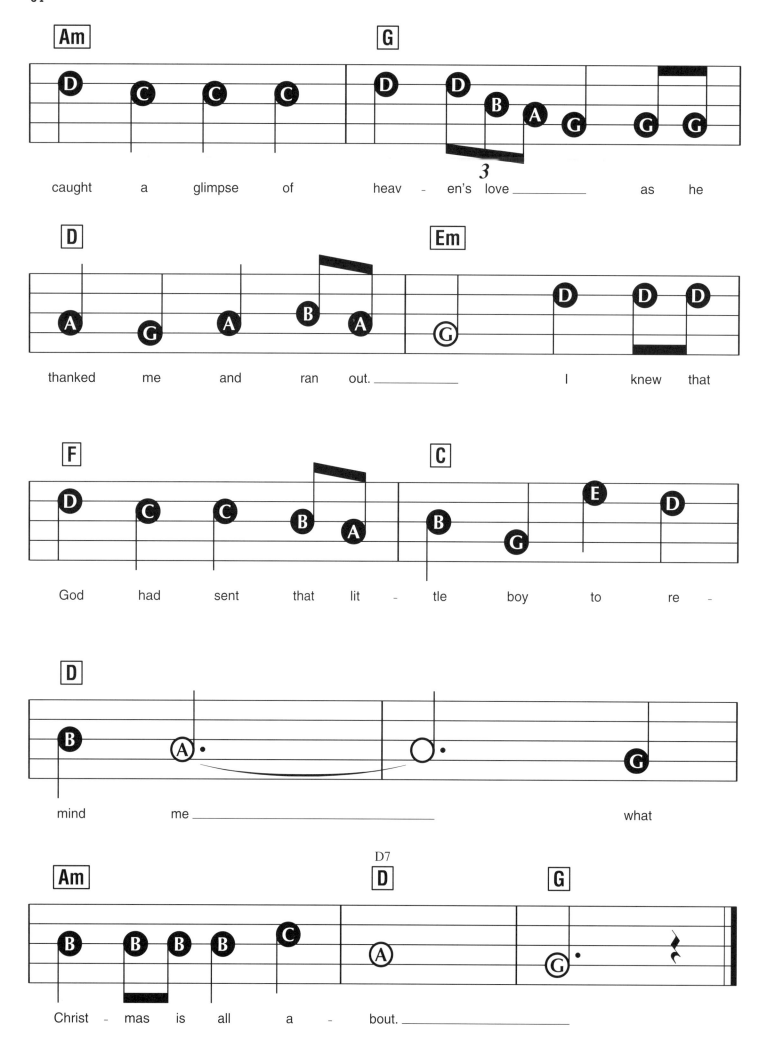

Do You Hear What I Hear

Registration 4

Words and Music by Noel Regney
and Gloria Shayne

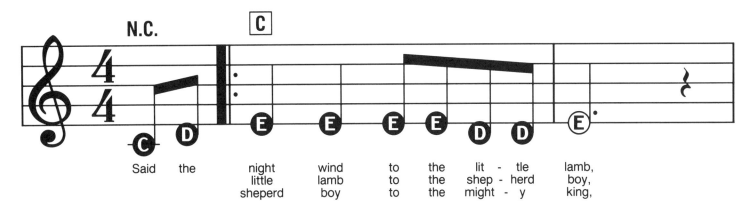

Said the night wind to the lit - tle lamb,
little lamb to the shep - herd boy,
sheperd boy to the might - y king,

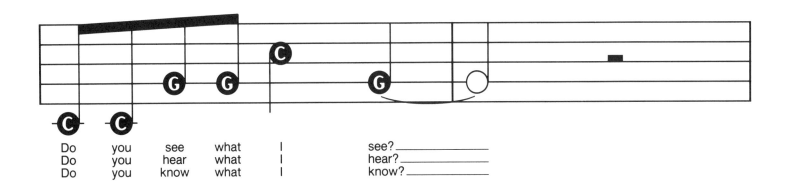

Do you see what I see?
Do you hear what I hear?
Do you know what I know?

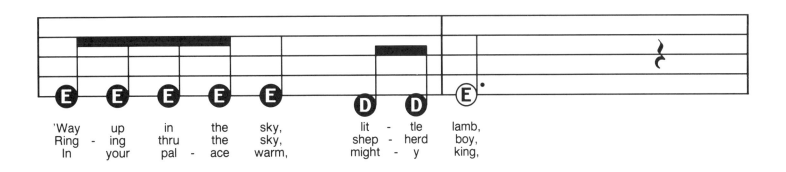

'Way up in the sky, lit - tle lamb,
Ring - ing thru the sky, shep - herd boy,
In your pal - ace warm, might - y king,

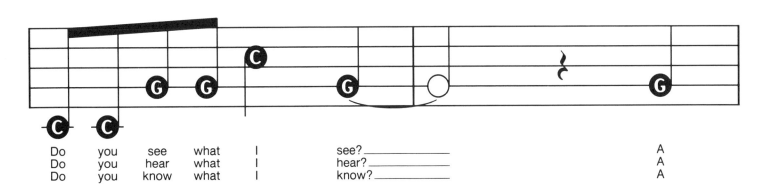

Do you see what I see?
Do you hear what I hear?
Do you know what I know?

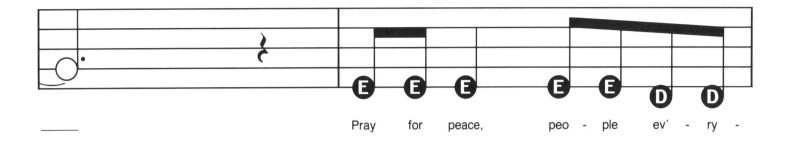

Pray   for   peace,   peo - ple   ev' - ry -

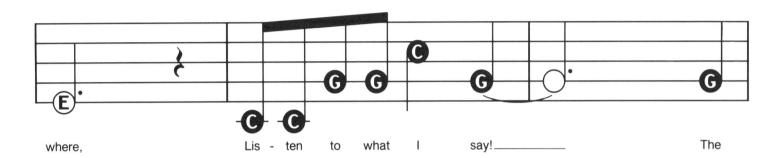

where,   Lis - ten   to   what   I   say! _____   The

Am   **Em**

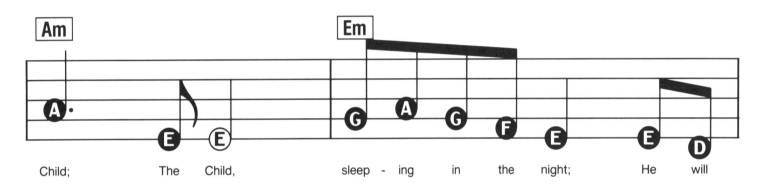

Child;   The   Child,   sleep - ing   in   the   night;   He   will

F   **G**   **E**   **G**   **F**

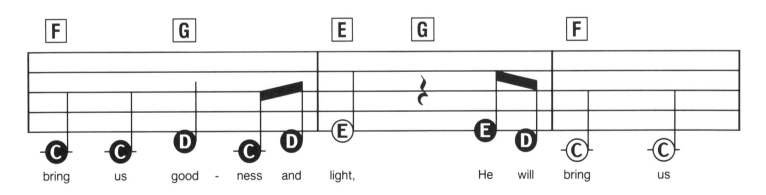

bring   us   good - ness   and   light,   He   will   bring   us

G7

G   **C**

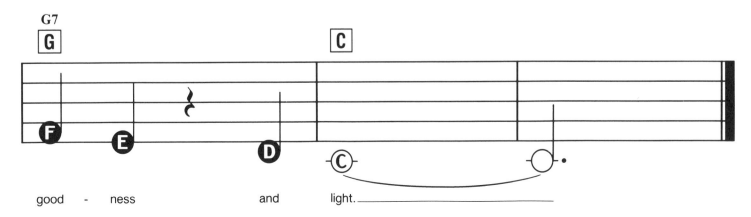

good - ness   and   light. _____

The Christmas Song
(Chestnuts Roasting on an Open Fire)

Registration 2
Rhythm: Ballad or Fox Trot

Music and Lyric by Mel Torme
and Robert Wells

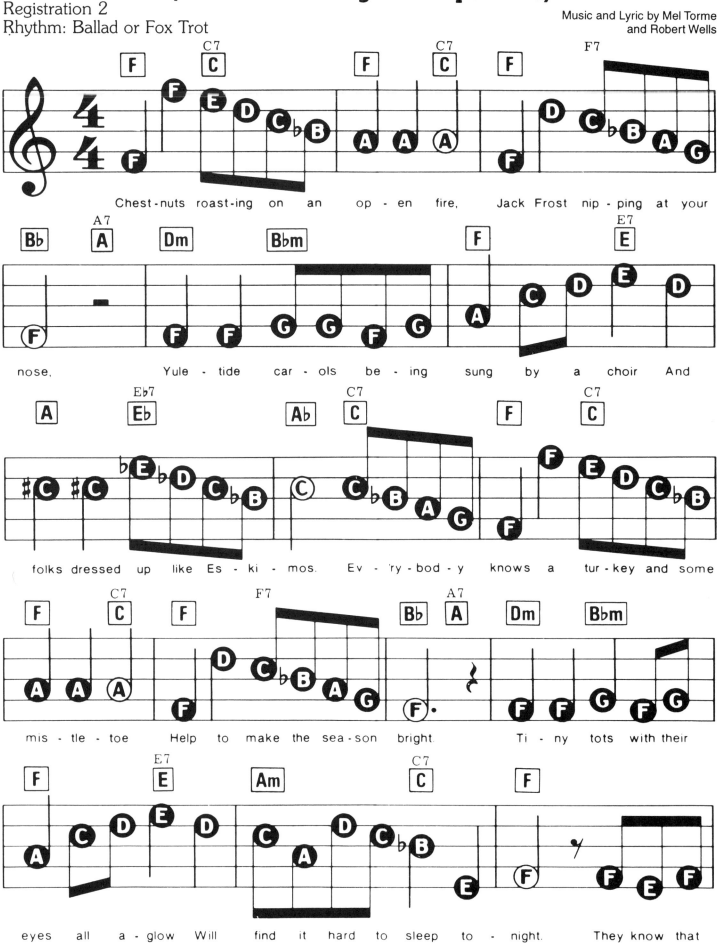

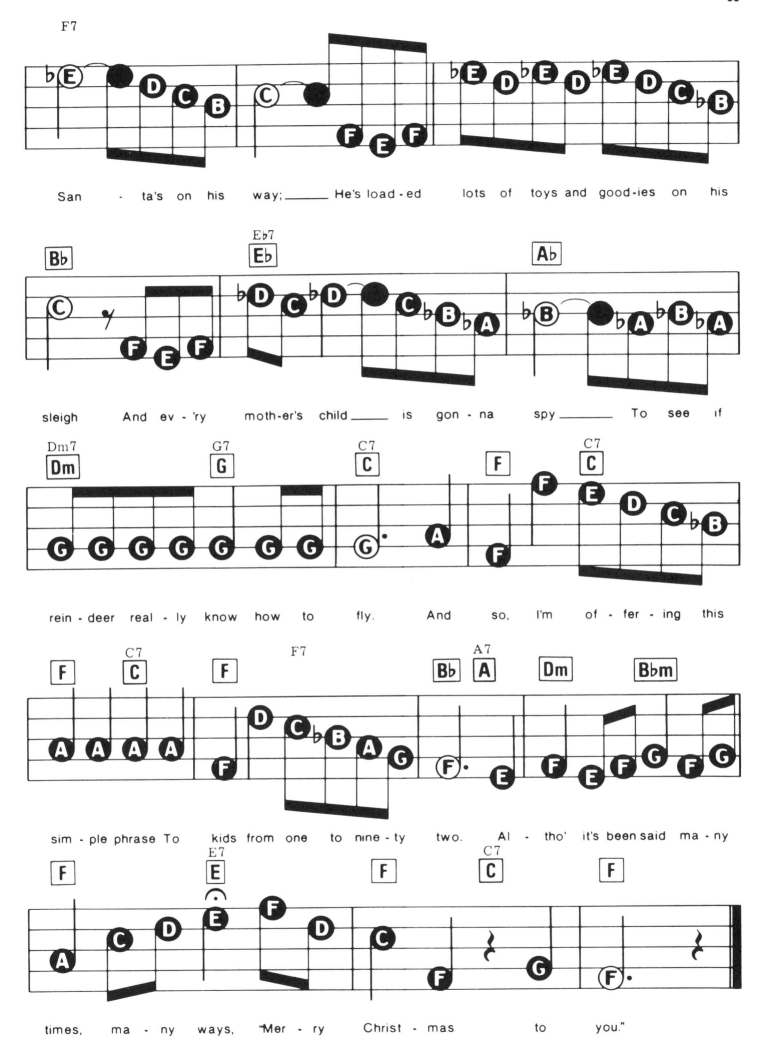

Christmas Time Is Here
from A CHARLIE BROWN CHRISTMAS

Registration 8
Rhythm: Waltz

Words by Lee Mendelson
Music by Vince Guaraldi

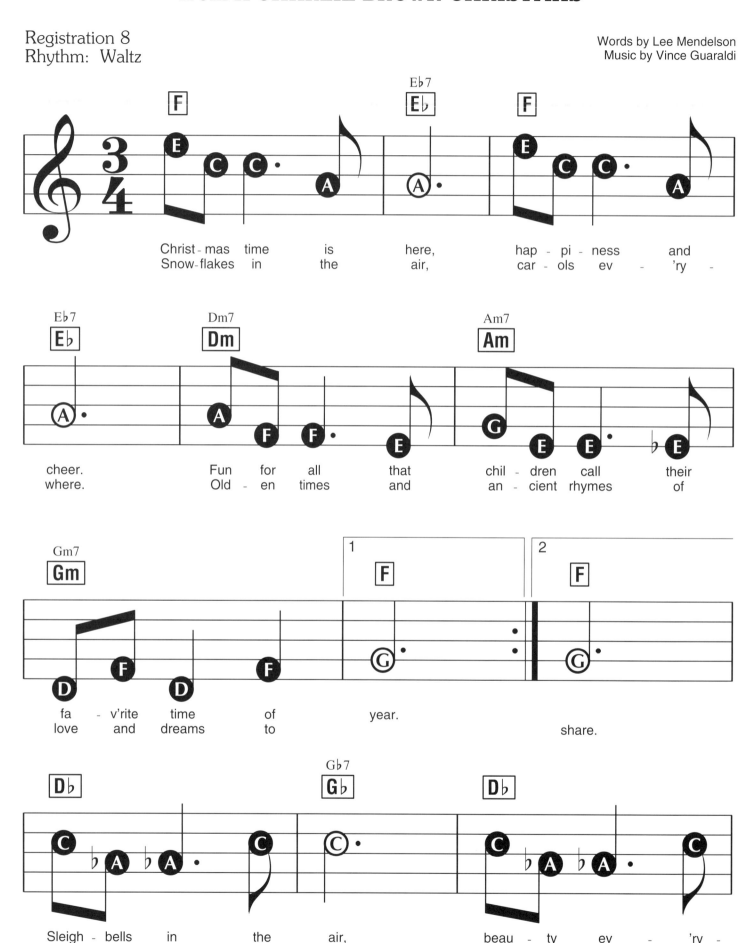

41

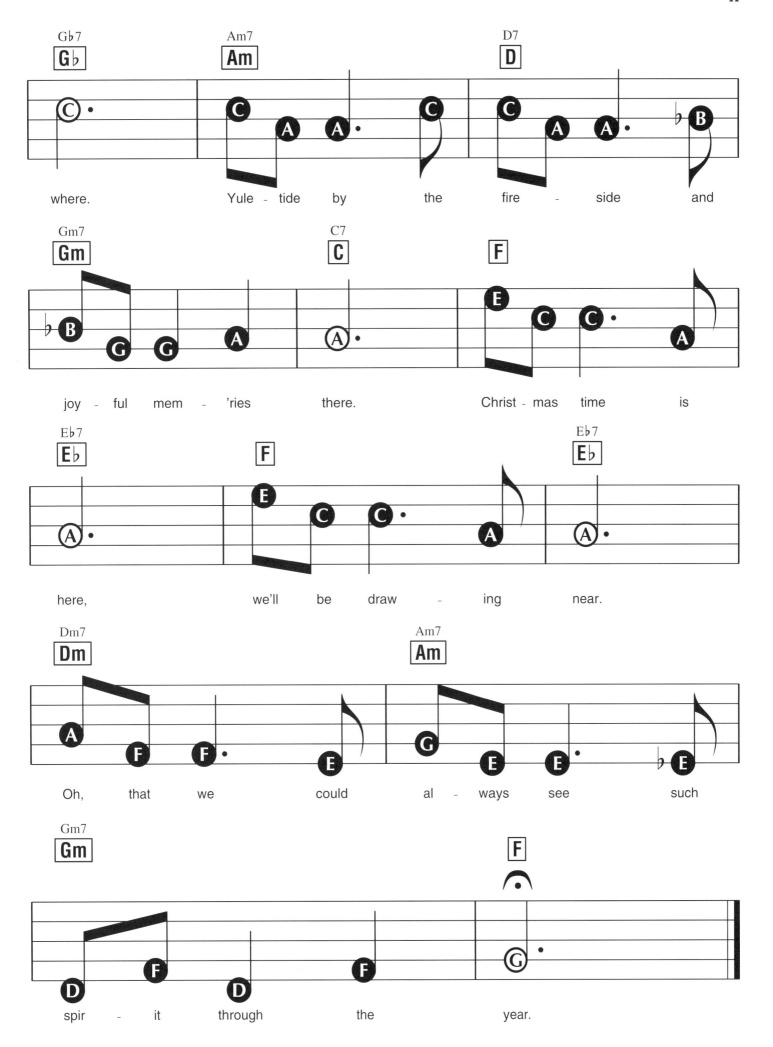

Emmanuel

Registration 4
Rhythm: Rock

Words and Music by
Michael W. Smith

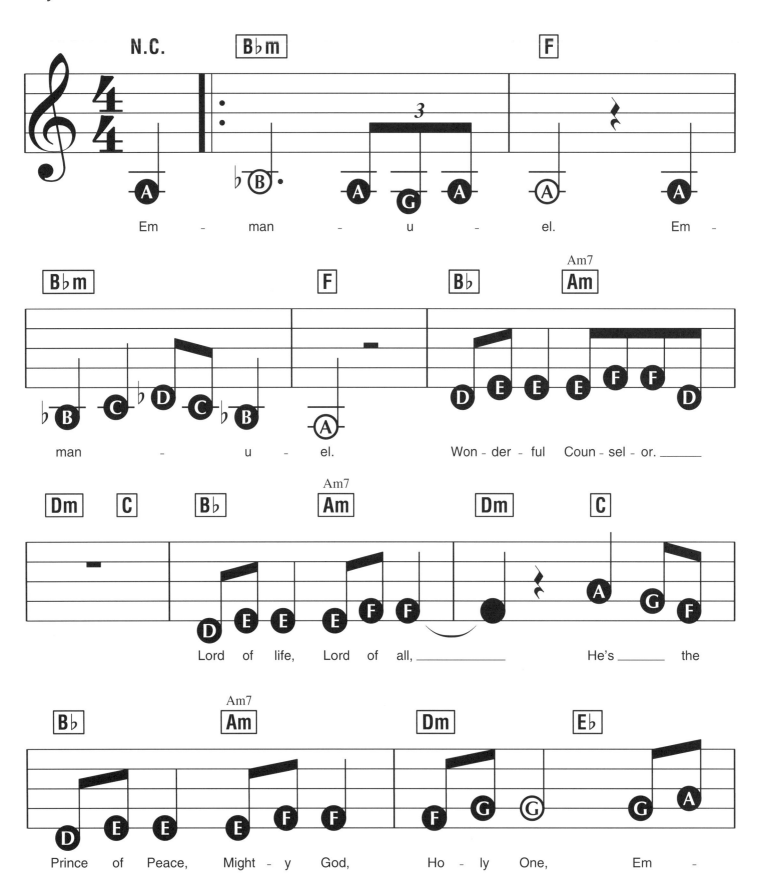

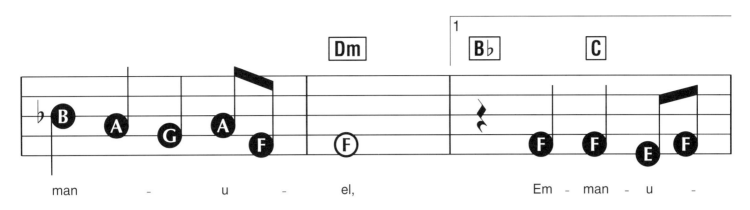

man - u - el,   Em - man - u -

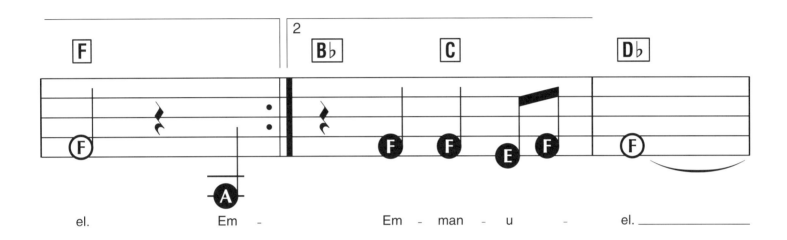

el.   Em -   Em - man - u - el. _____

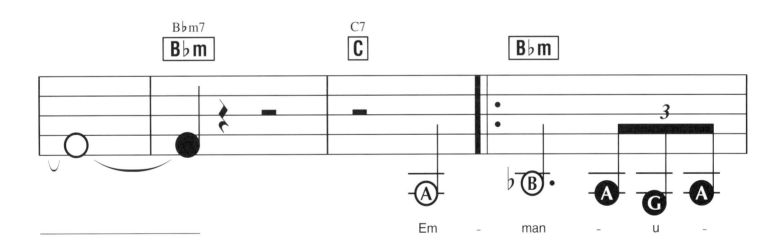

Em - man - u -

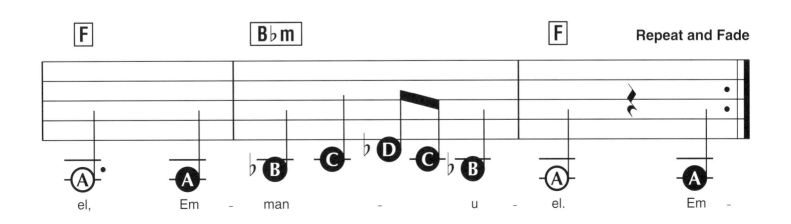

el,   Em - man - u - el.   Em -

Feliz Navidad

Registration 1
Rhythm: Latin or Bossa Nova

Music and Lyrics by
José Feliciano

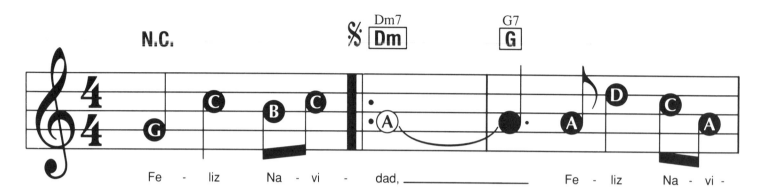

Fe - liz Na - vi - dad, _____ Fe - liz Na - vi -

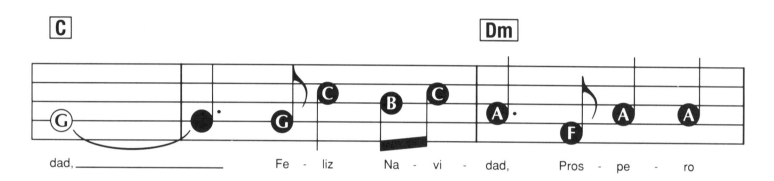

dad, _____ Fe - liz Na - vi - dad, Pros - pe - ro

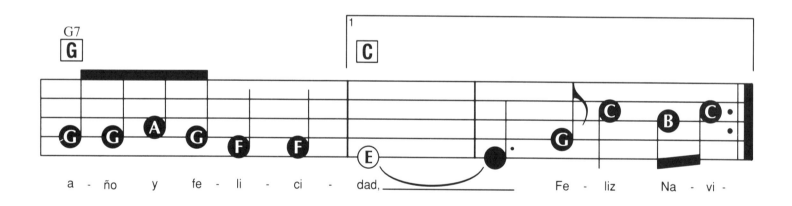

a - ño y fe - li - ci - dad, _____ Fe - liz Na - vi -

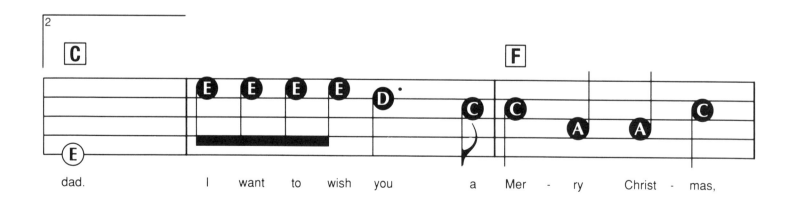

dad. I want to wish you a Mer - ry Christ - mas,

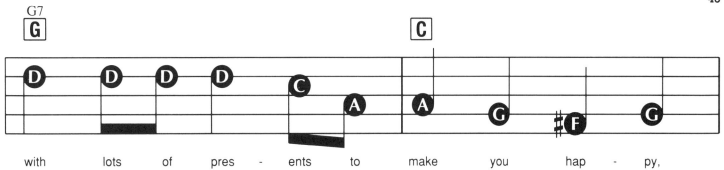

with lots of pres - ents to make you hap - py,

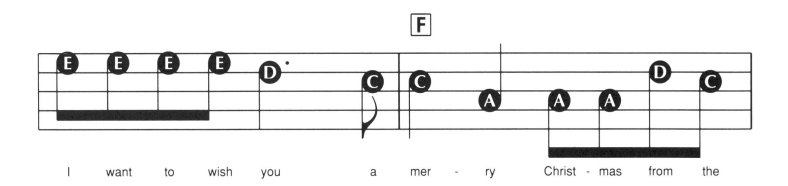

I want to wish you a mer - ry Christ - mas from the

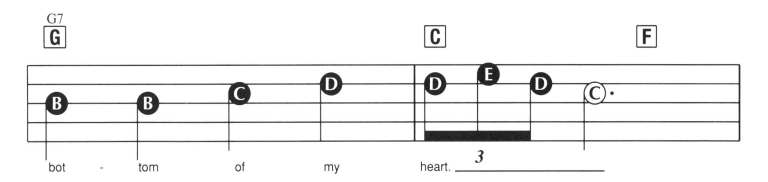

bot - tom of my heart. _____

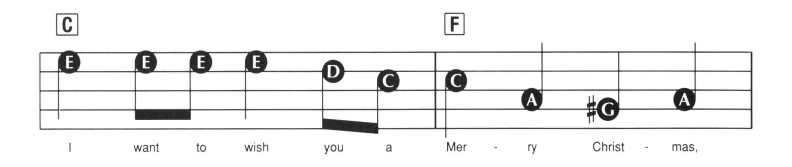

I want to wish you a Mer - ry Christ - mas,

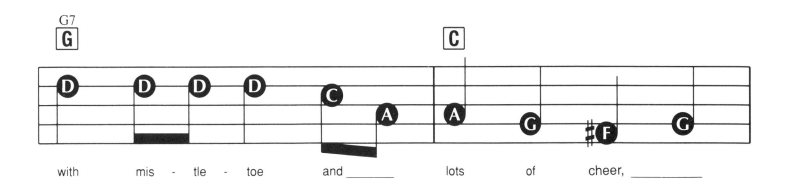

with mis - tle - toe and _____ lots of cheer, _____

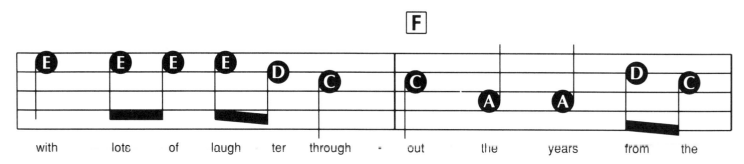

with lots of laugh - ter through - out the years from the

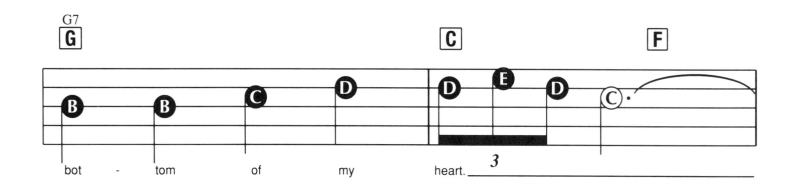

bot - tom of my heart.

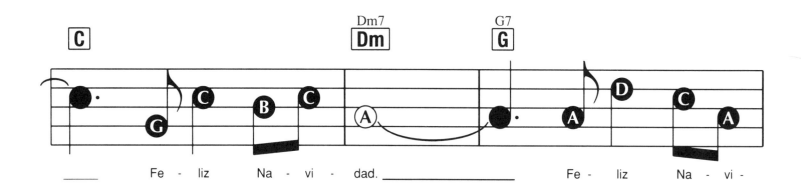

____ Fe - liz Na - vi - dad. ____ Fe - liz Na - vi -

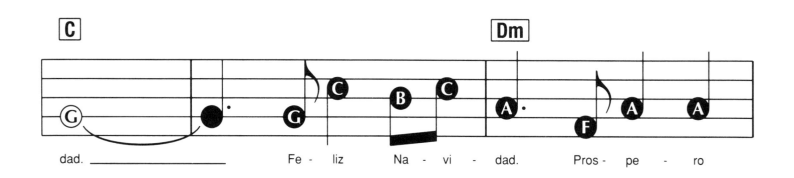

dad. ____ Fe - liz Na - vi - dad. Pros - pe - ro

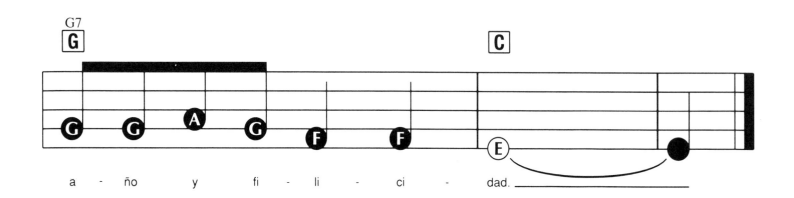

a - ño y fi - li - ci - dad. ____

The Gift

Registration 9
Rhythm: Ballad

Words and Music by Tom Douglas
and Jim Brickman

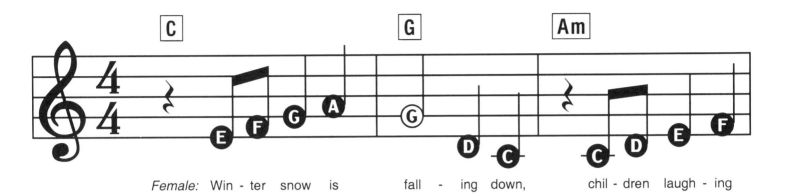

Female: Win - ter snow is fall - ing down, chil - dren laugh - ing

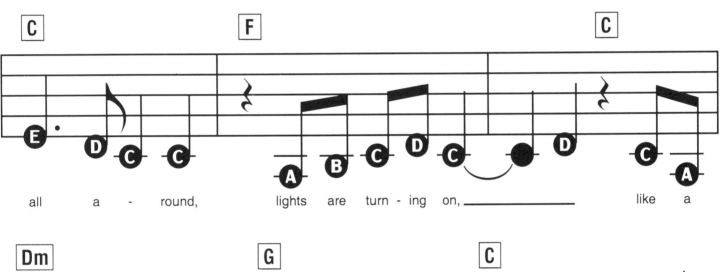

all a - round, lights are turn - ing on, _____ like a

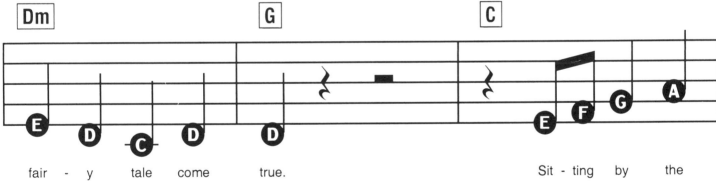

fair - y tale come true. Sit - ting by the

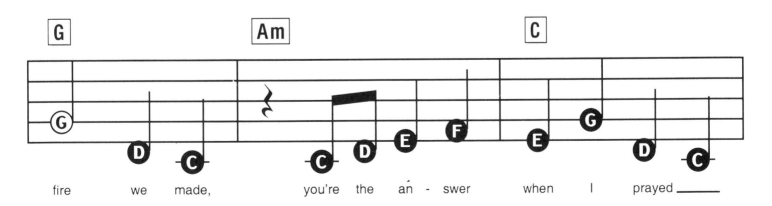

fire we made, you're the an - swer when I prayed _____

48

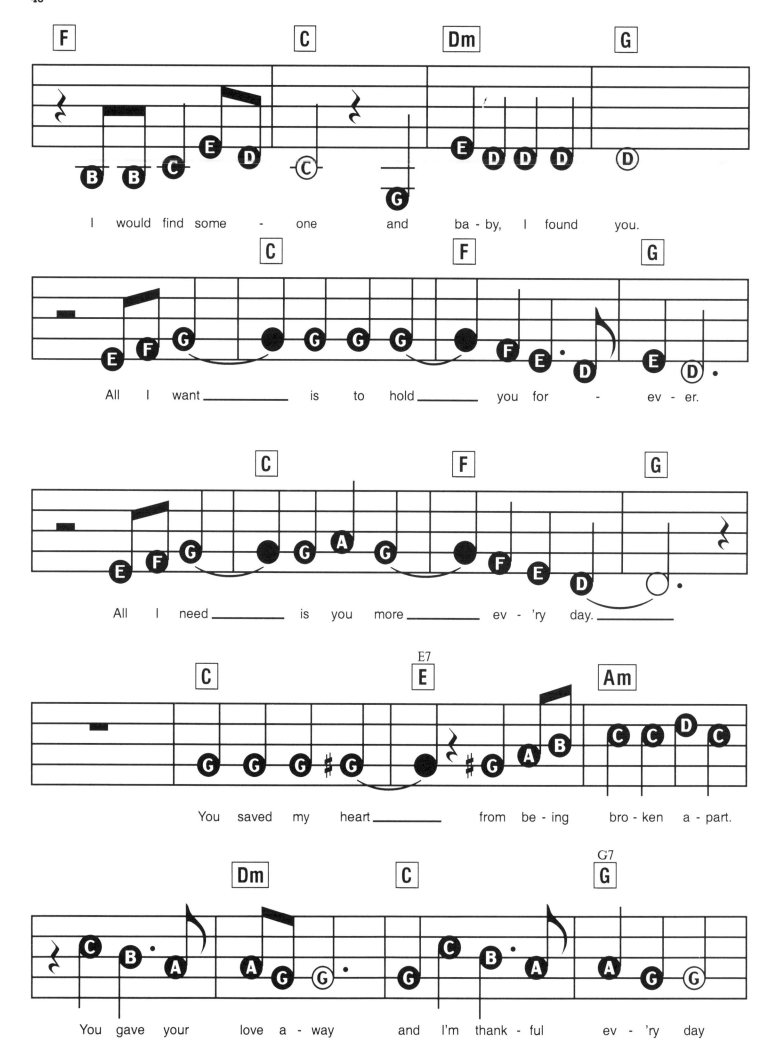

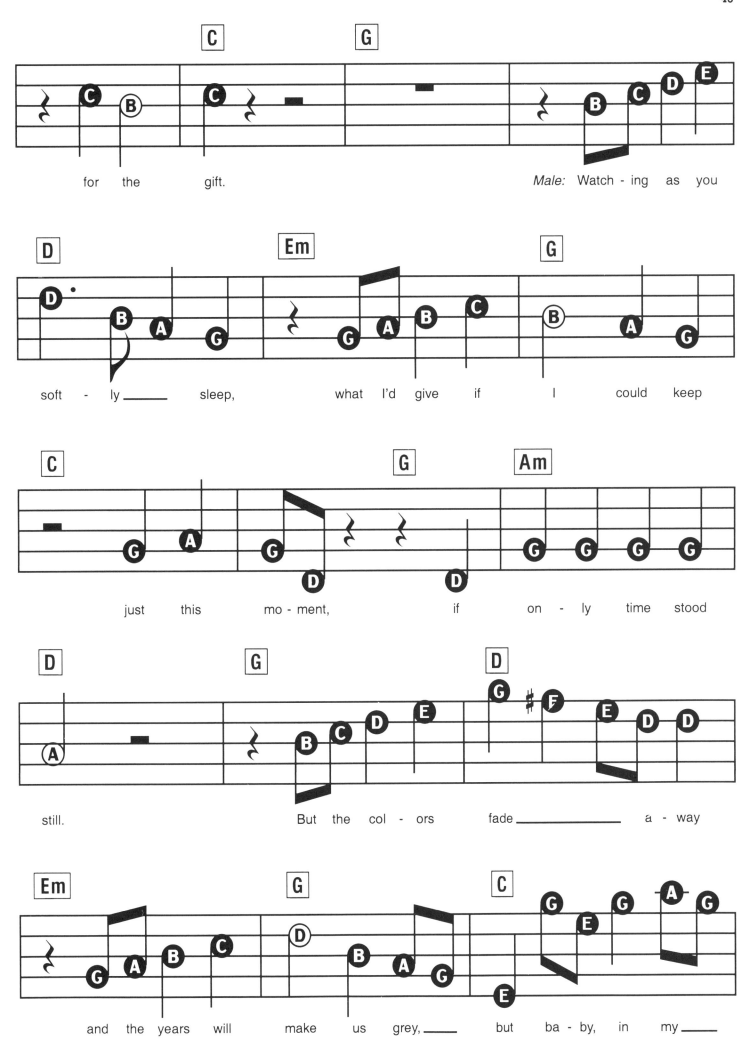

49

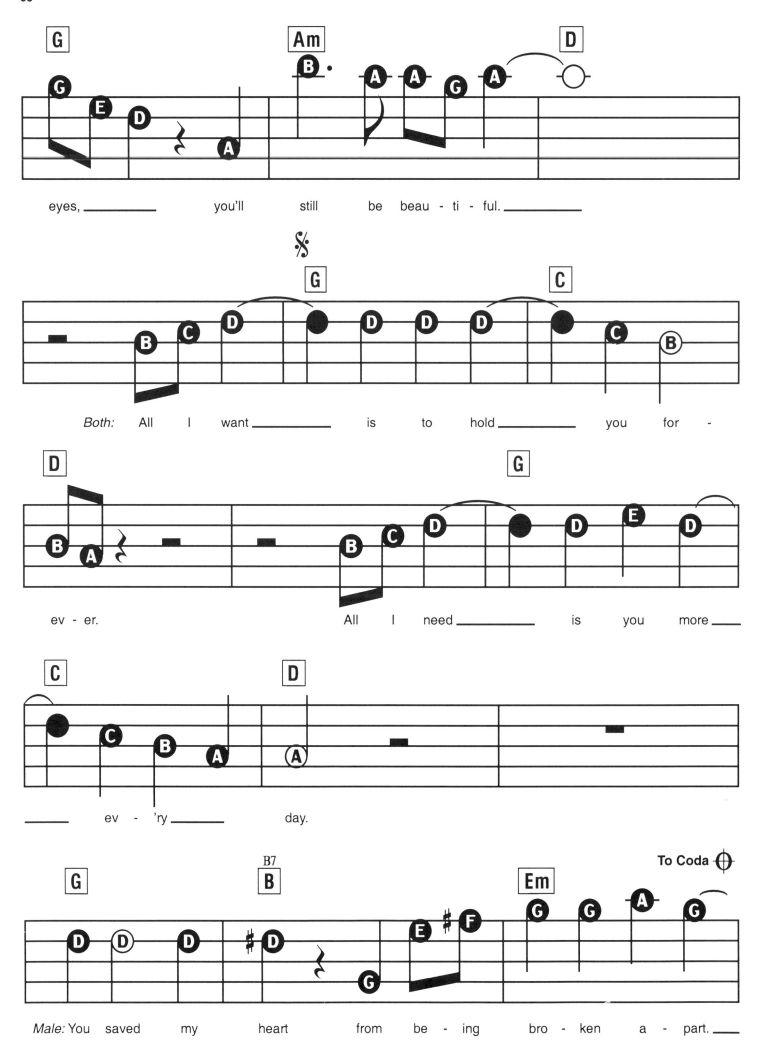

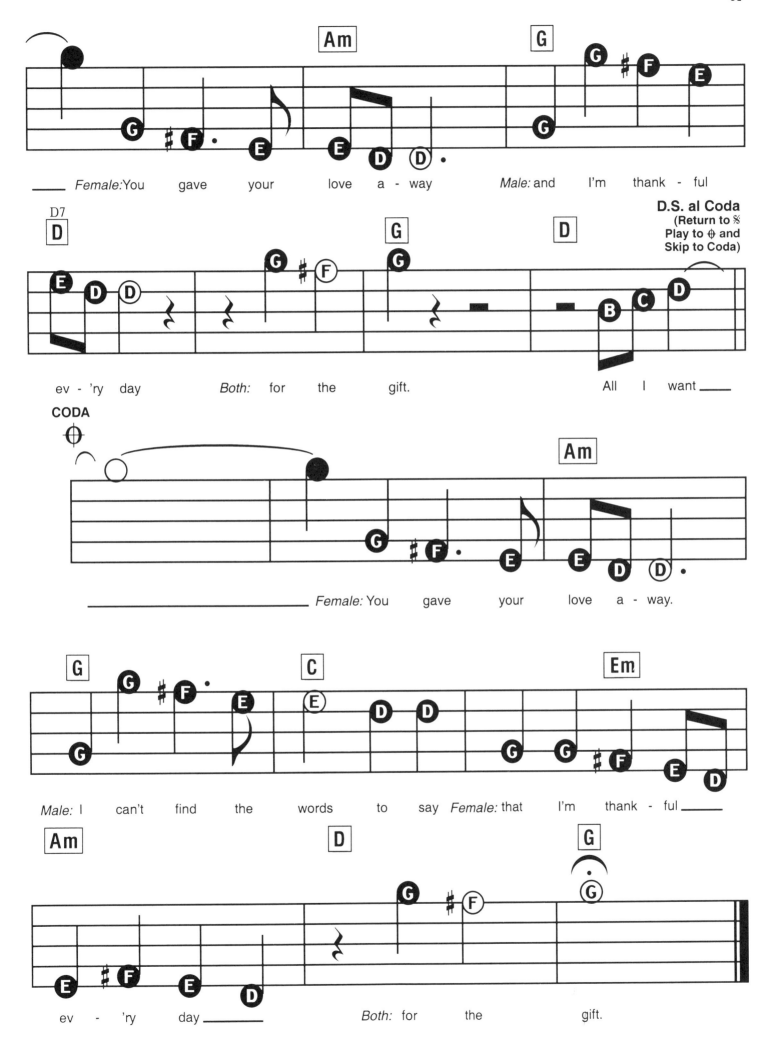

Grown-Up Christmas List

Registration 1
Rhythm: 4/4 Ballad

Words and Music by David Foster
and Linda Thompson-Jenner

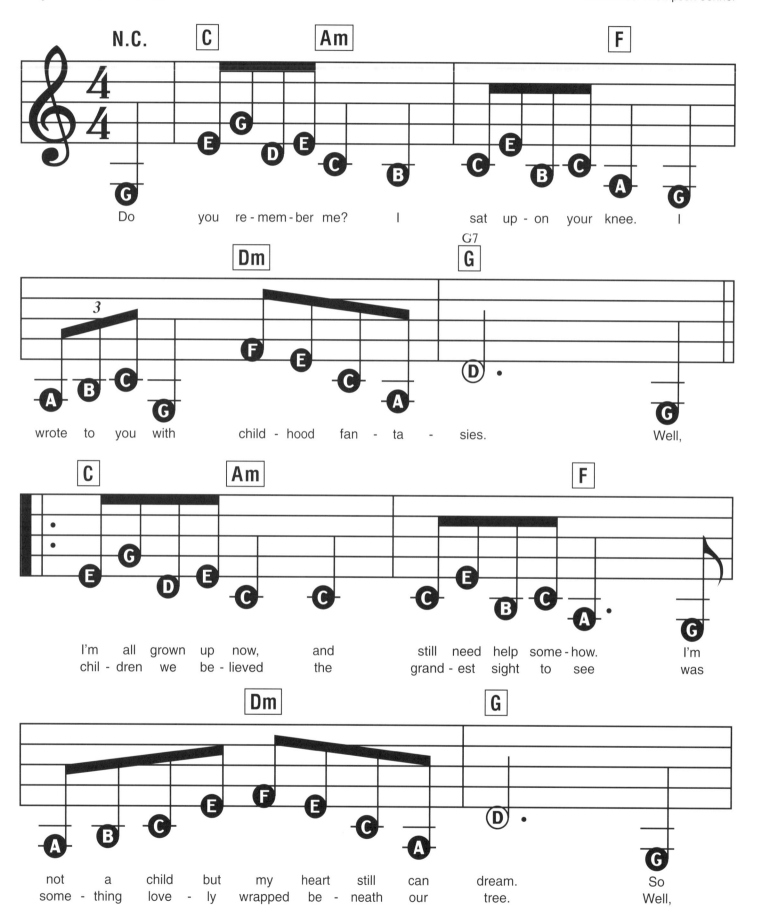

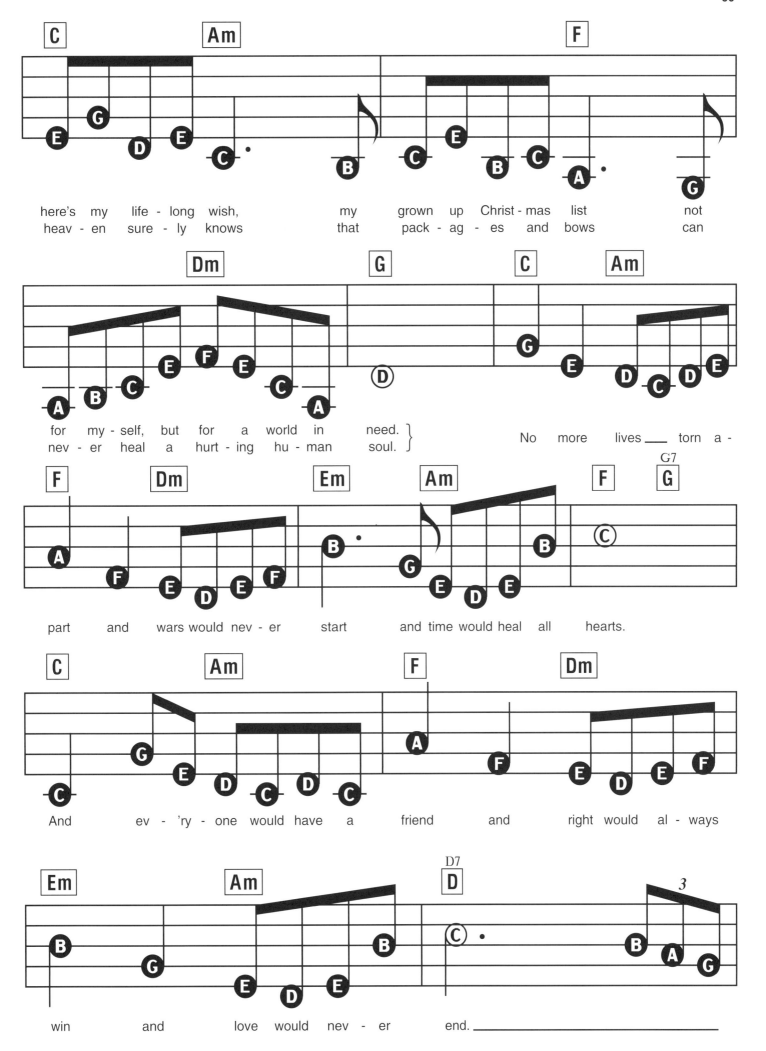

54

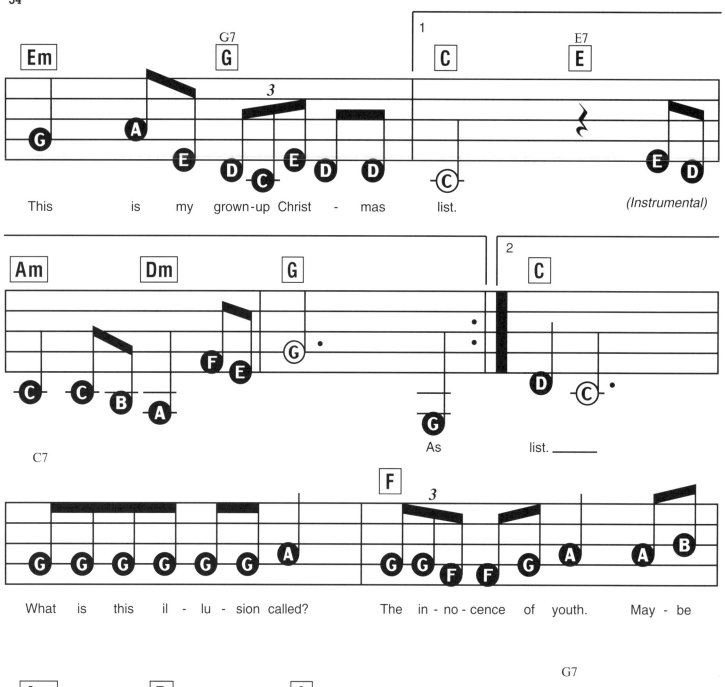

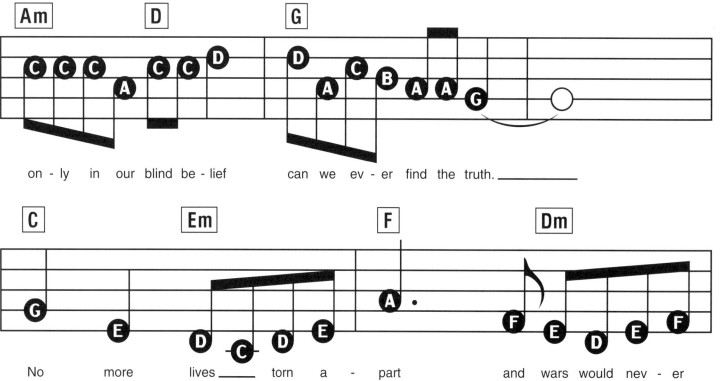

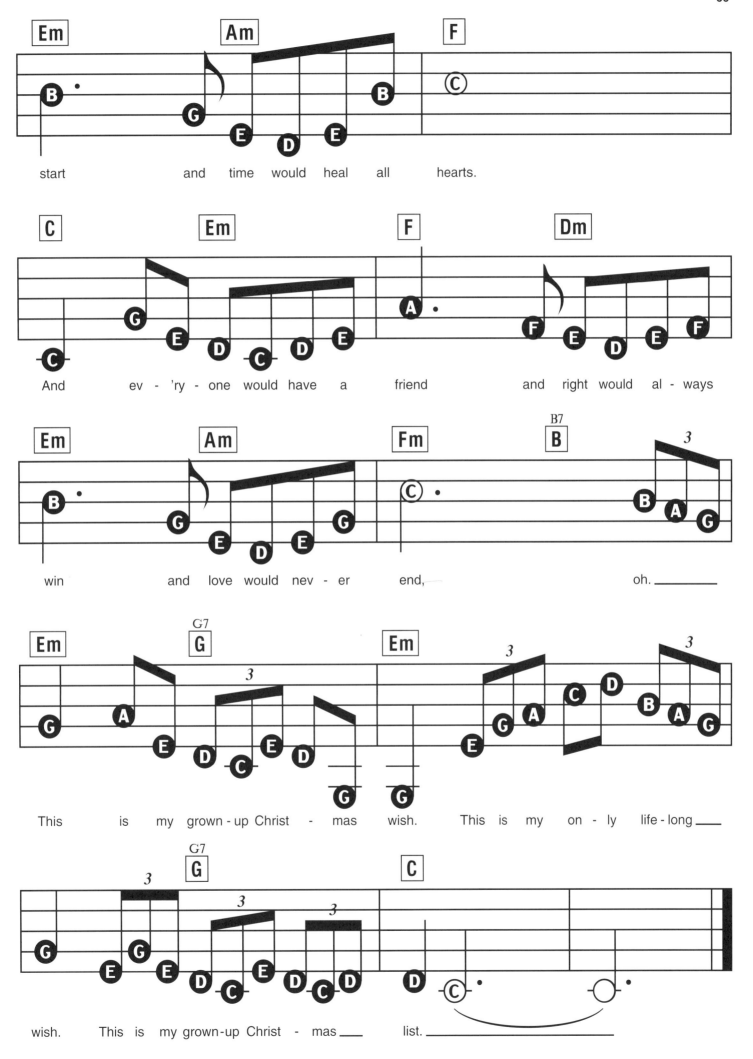

Holly Leaves and Christmas Trees

Registration 10
Rhythm: 4/4 Ballad

Words and Music by Red West
and Glen Spreen

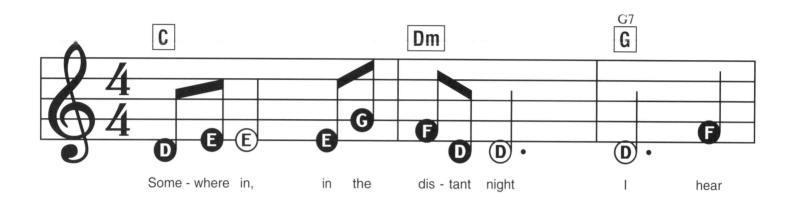

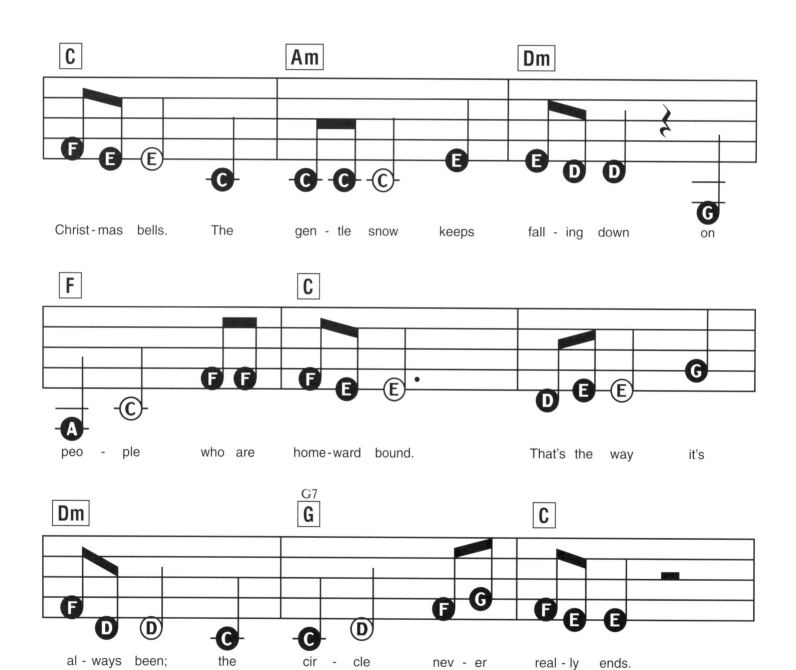

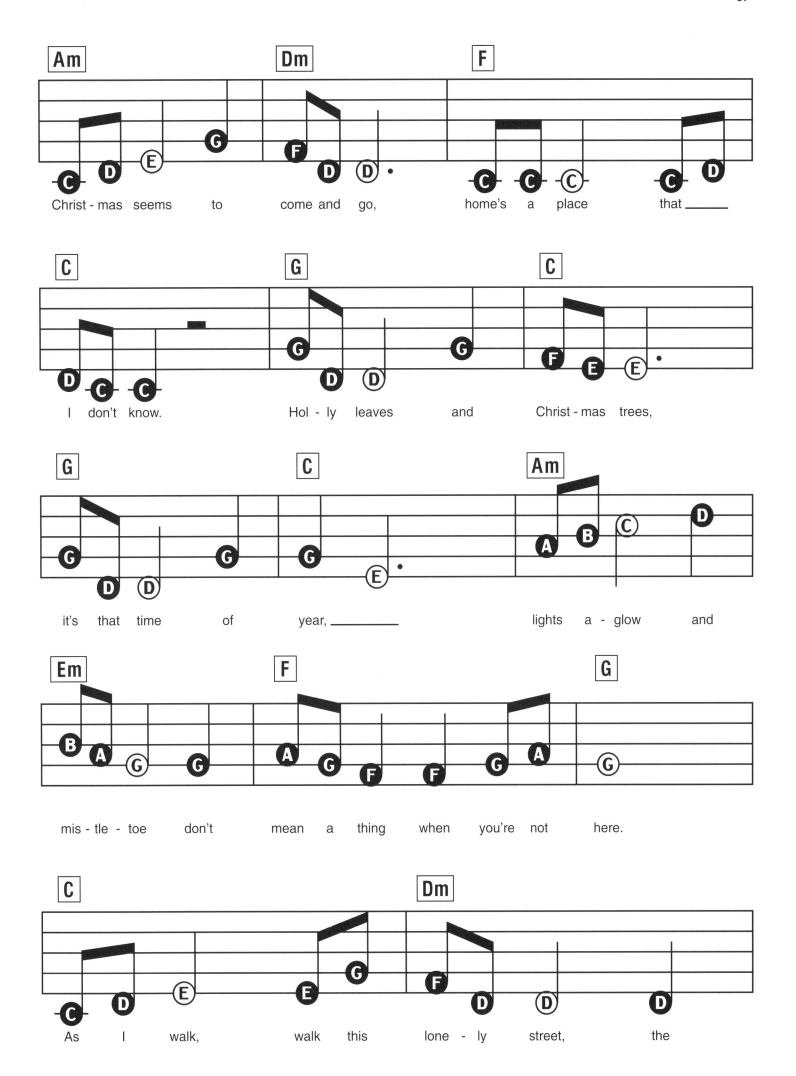

(Instrumental)

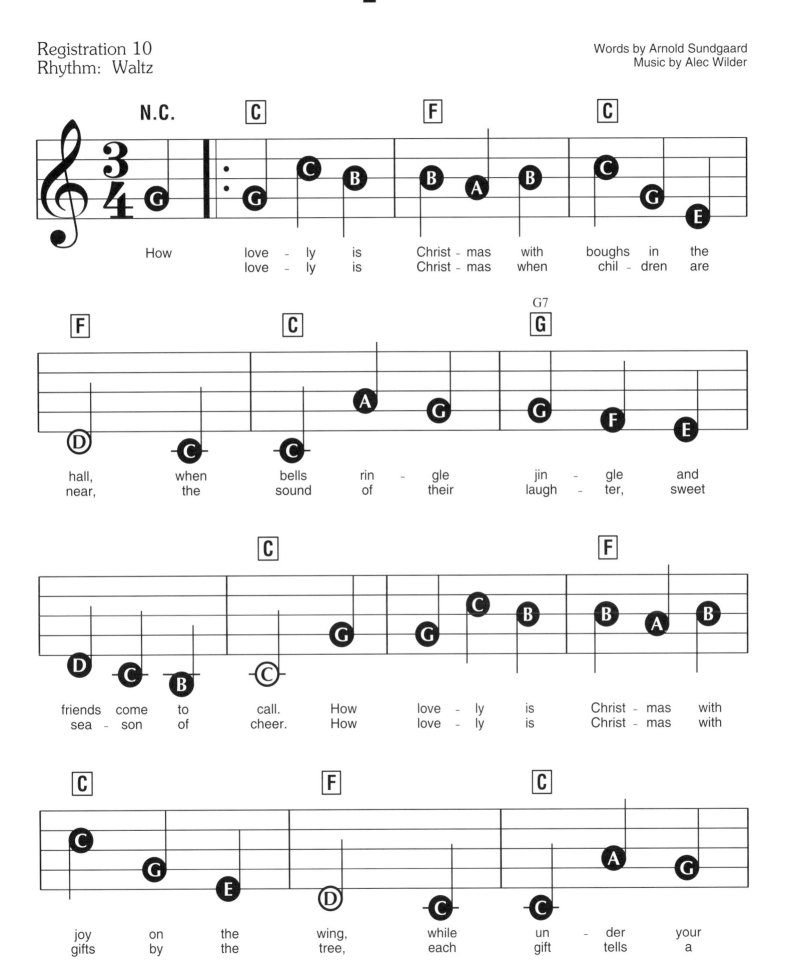

How Lovely Is Christmas

Registration 10
Rhythm: Waltz

Words by Arnold Sundgaard
Music by Alec Wilder

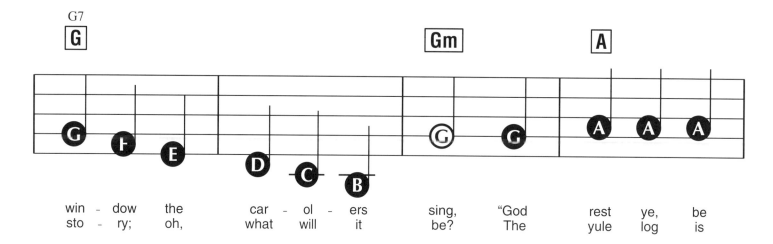

win - dow the car - ol - ers sing, "God rest ye, be
sto - ry; oh, what will it be? The yule log is

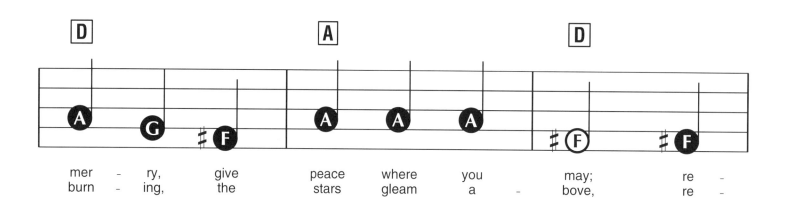

mer - ry, give the peace where you may; re -
burn - ing, give the stars gleam a - bove, re -

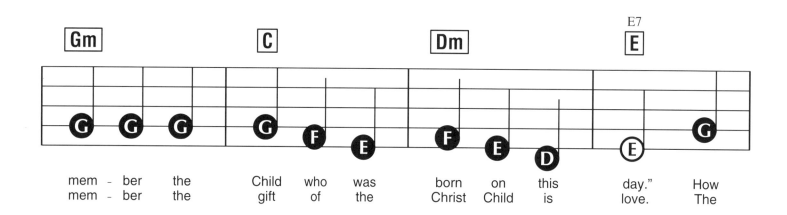

mem - ber the Child who was born on this day." How
mem - ber the gift of the Christ Child is love. The

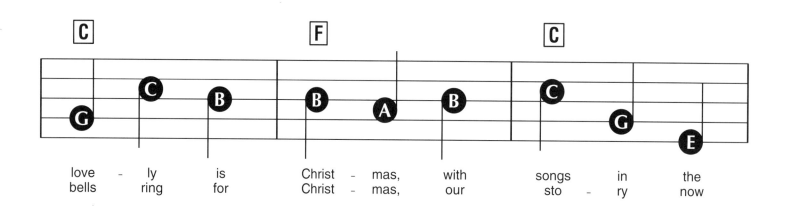

love - ly is Christ - mas, with songs in the
bells ring for Christ - mas, our sto - ry now

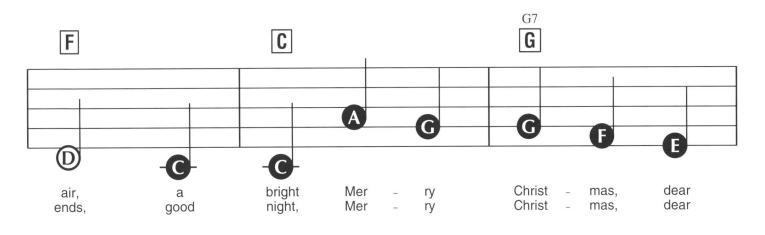

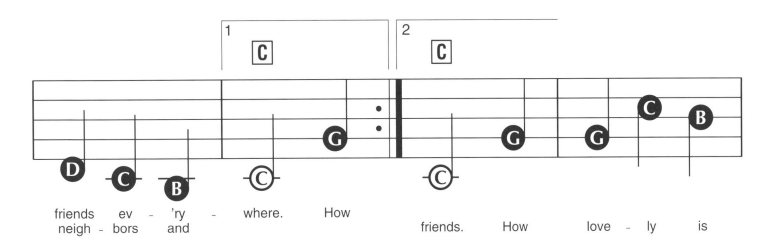

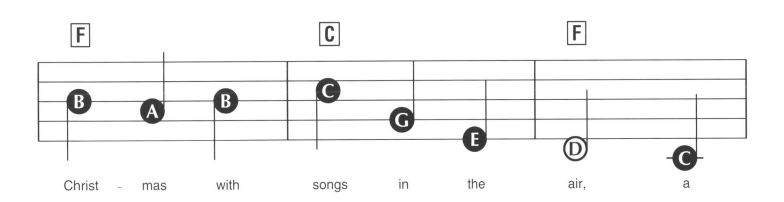

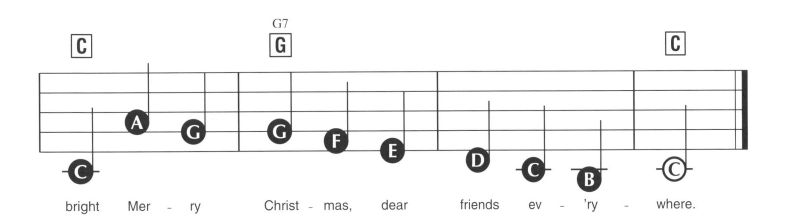

I Wonder as I Wander

Registration 1
Rhythm: Waltz

By John Jacob Niles

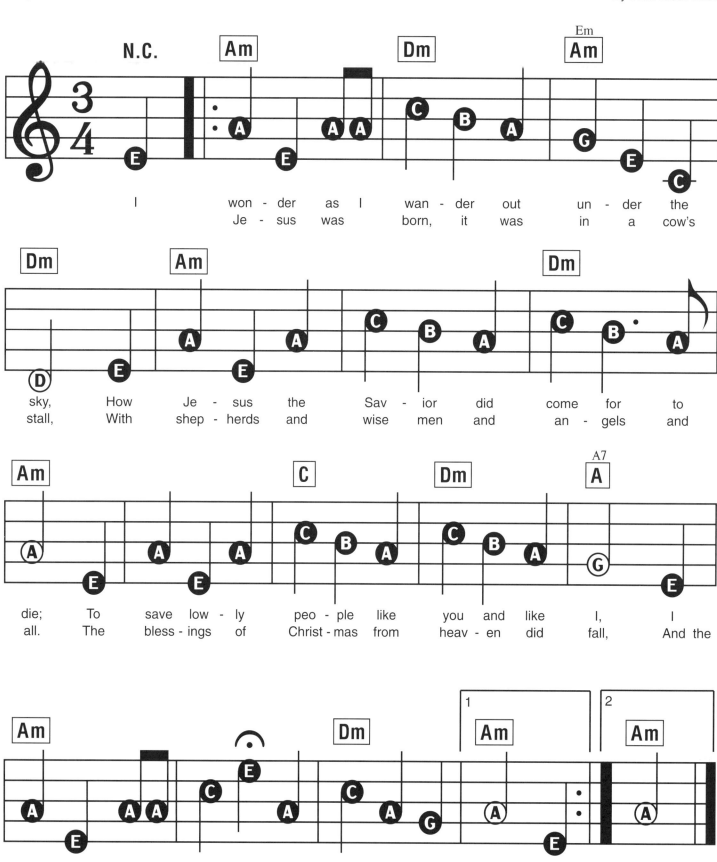

I'll Be Home on Christmas Day

Registration 8
Rhythm: 4/4 Ballad

Words and Music by
Michael Jarrett

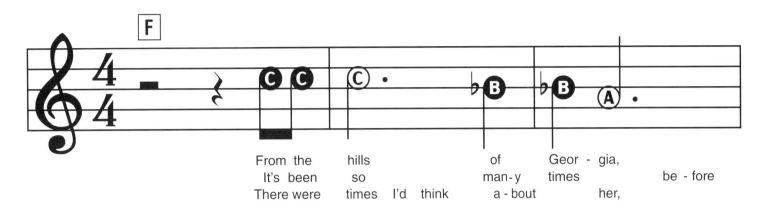

From the hills of Geor - gia,
It's been so man-y times be - fore
There were times I'd think a - bout her,

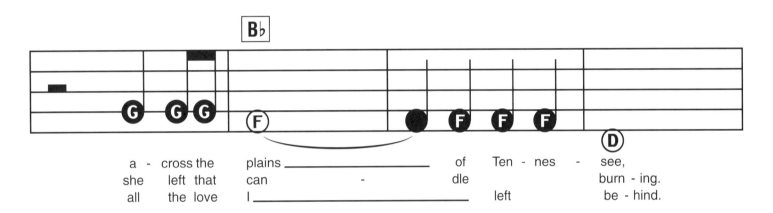

a - cross the plains of Ten - nes - see,
she left that can - dle burn - ing.
all the love I left be - hind.

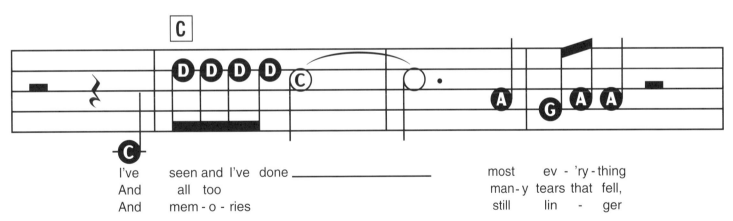

I've seen and I've done most ev - 'ry-thing
And all too man-y tears that fell,
And mem - o - ries still lin - ger

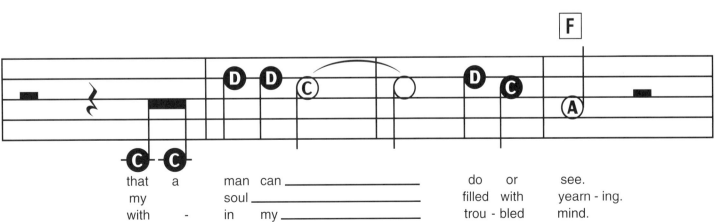

that a man can do or see.
my soul filled with yearn - ing.
with - in my trou - bled mind.

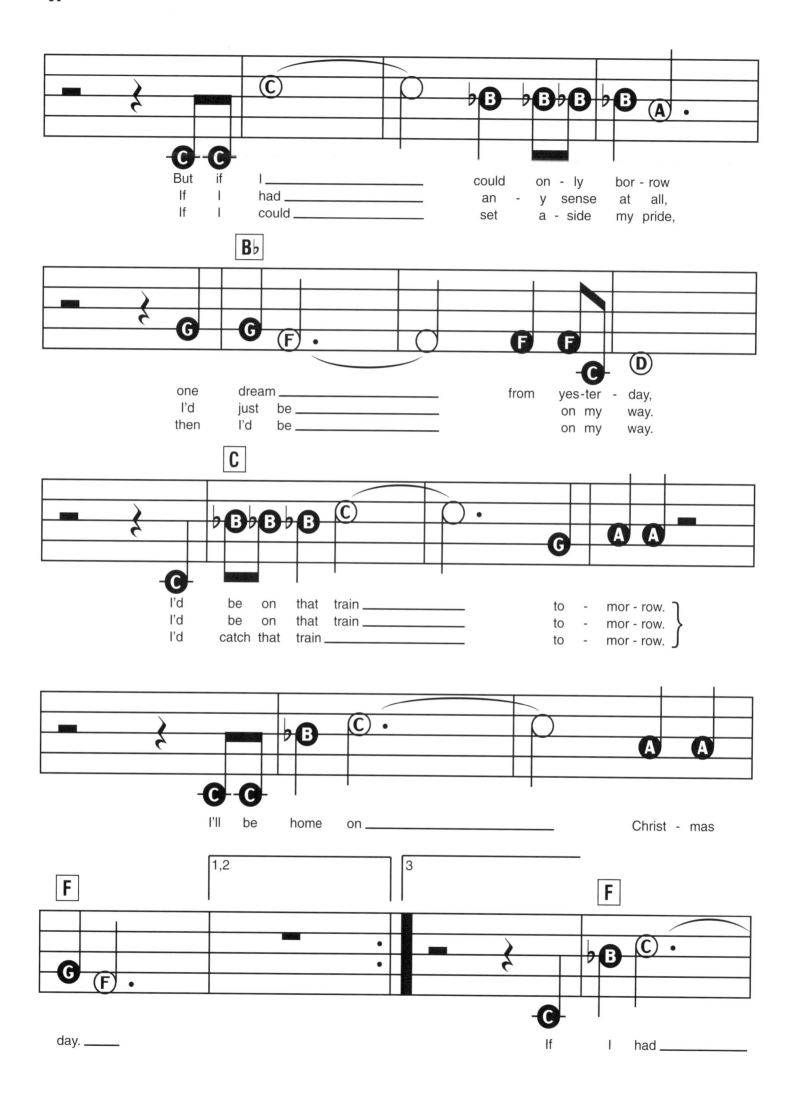

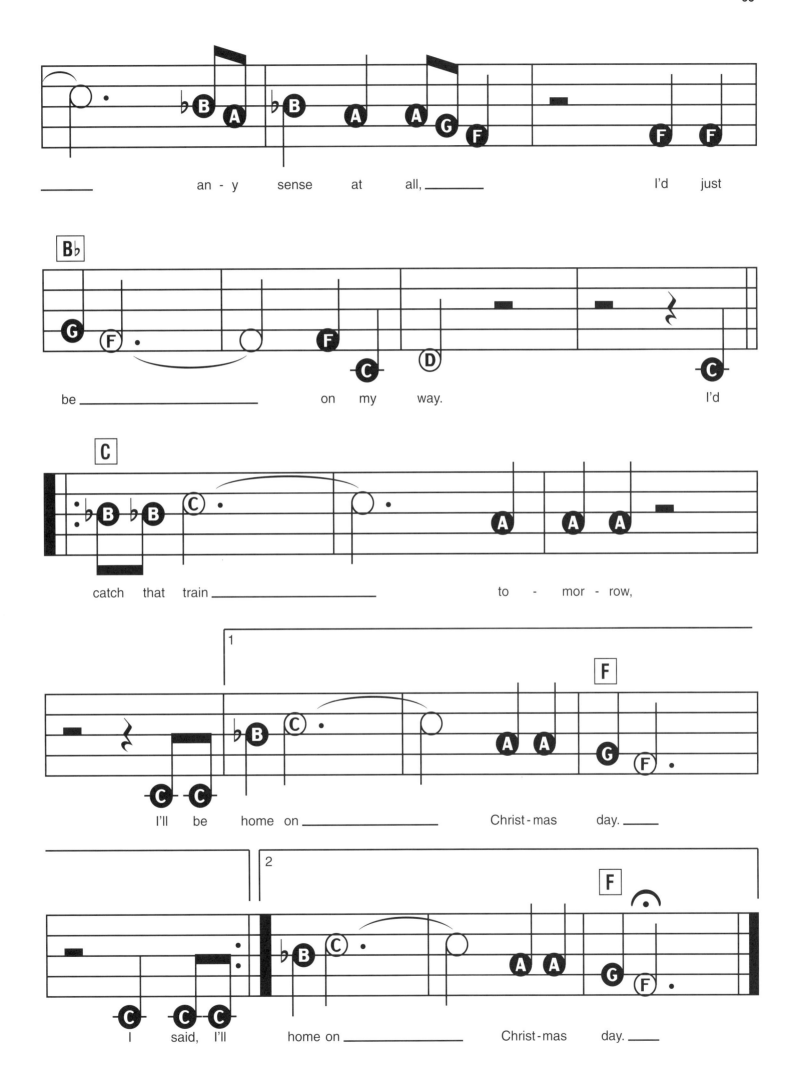

I'm Spending Christmas with You

Registration: 5
Rhythm: Waltz or Jazz Waltz

Words and Music by
Tom Occhipinti

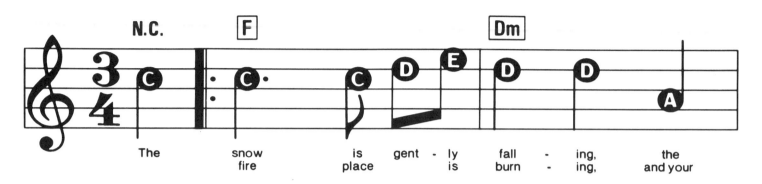

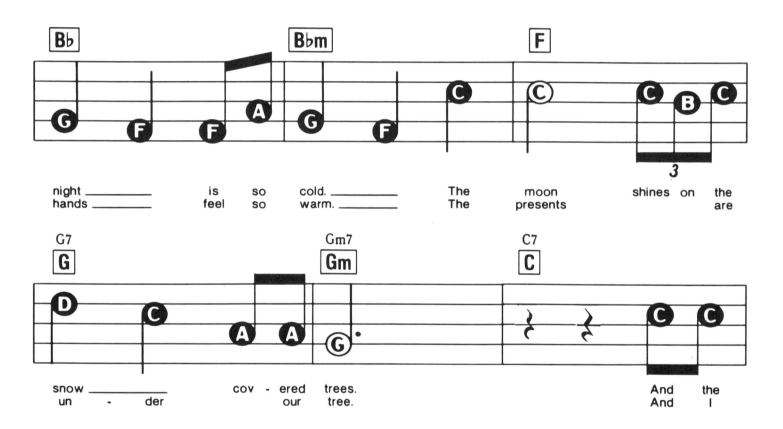

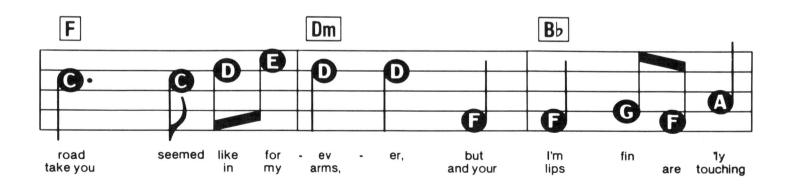

67

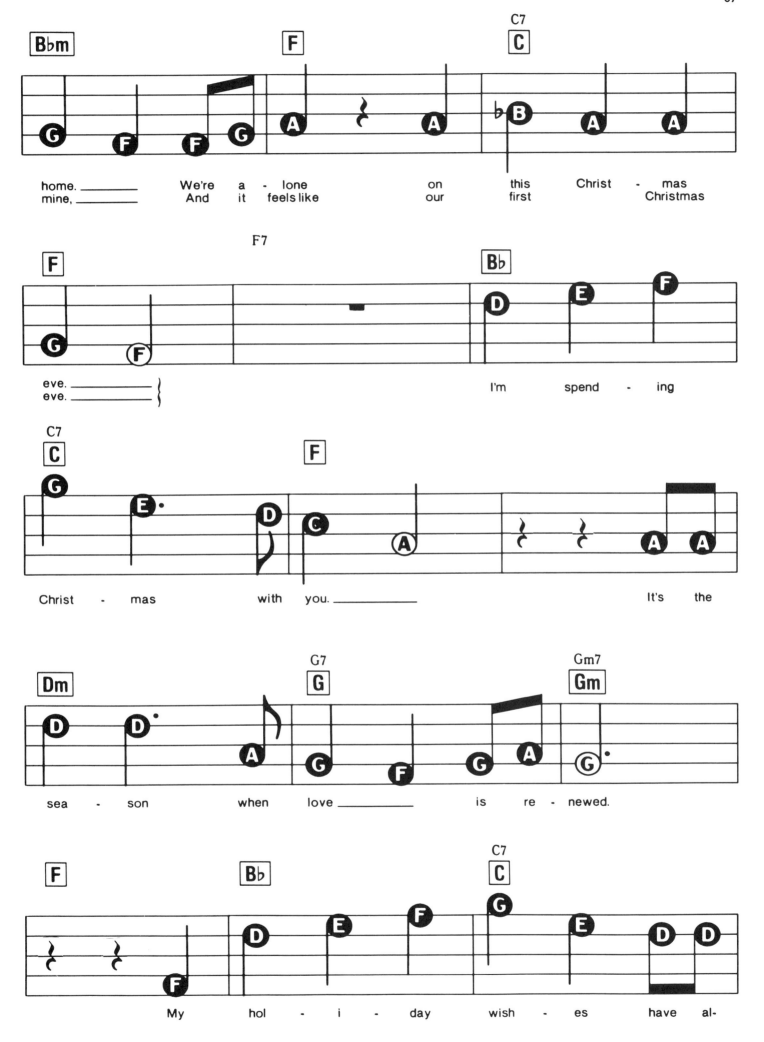

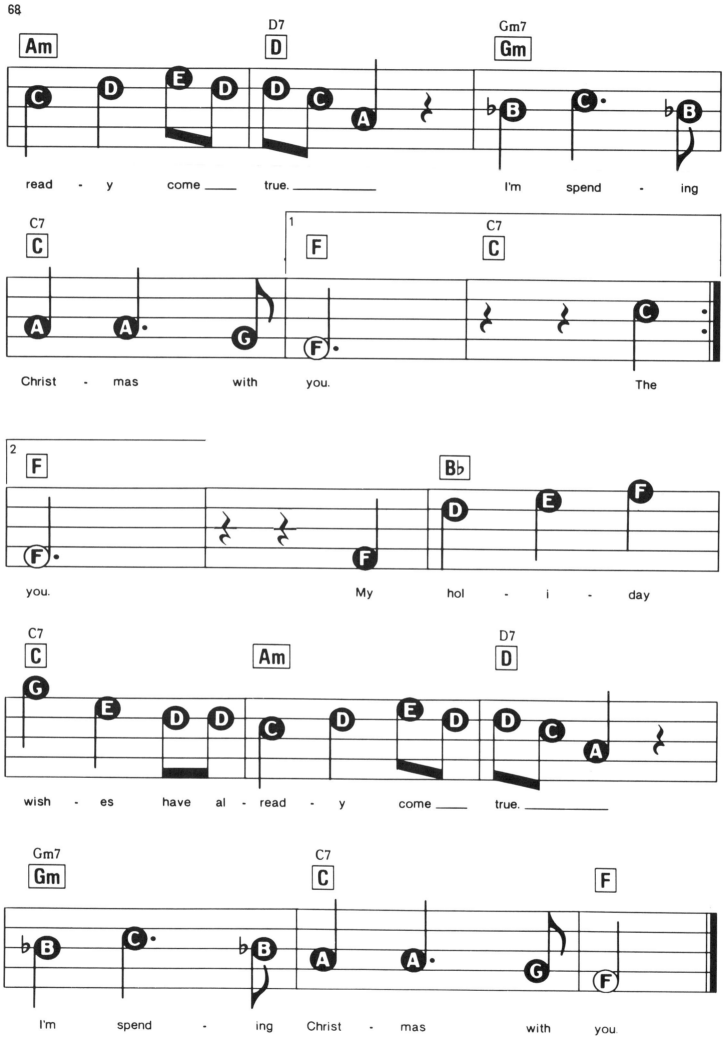

It's Beginning to Look Like Christmas

Registration 5
Rhythm: Fox Trot or Shuffle

By Meredith Willson

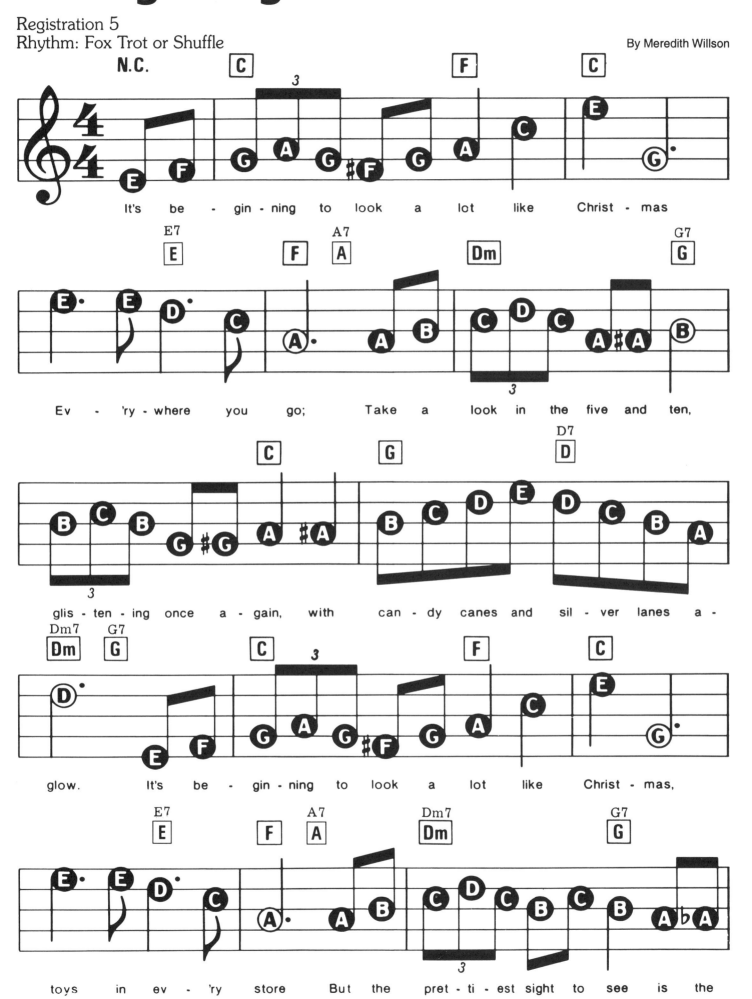

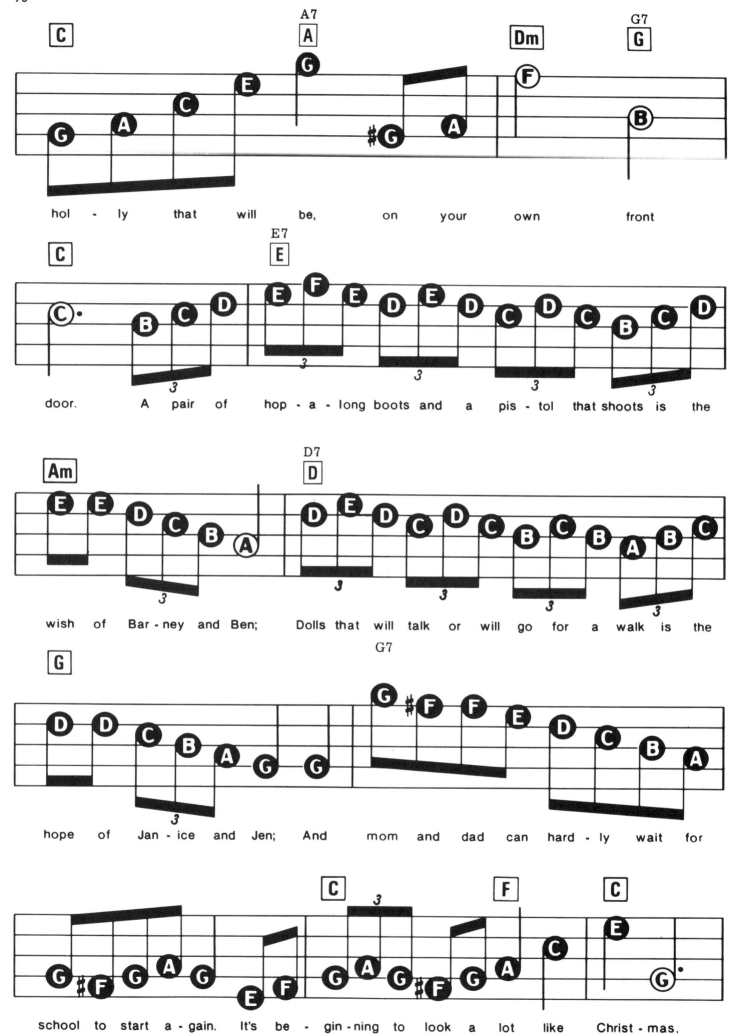

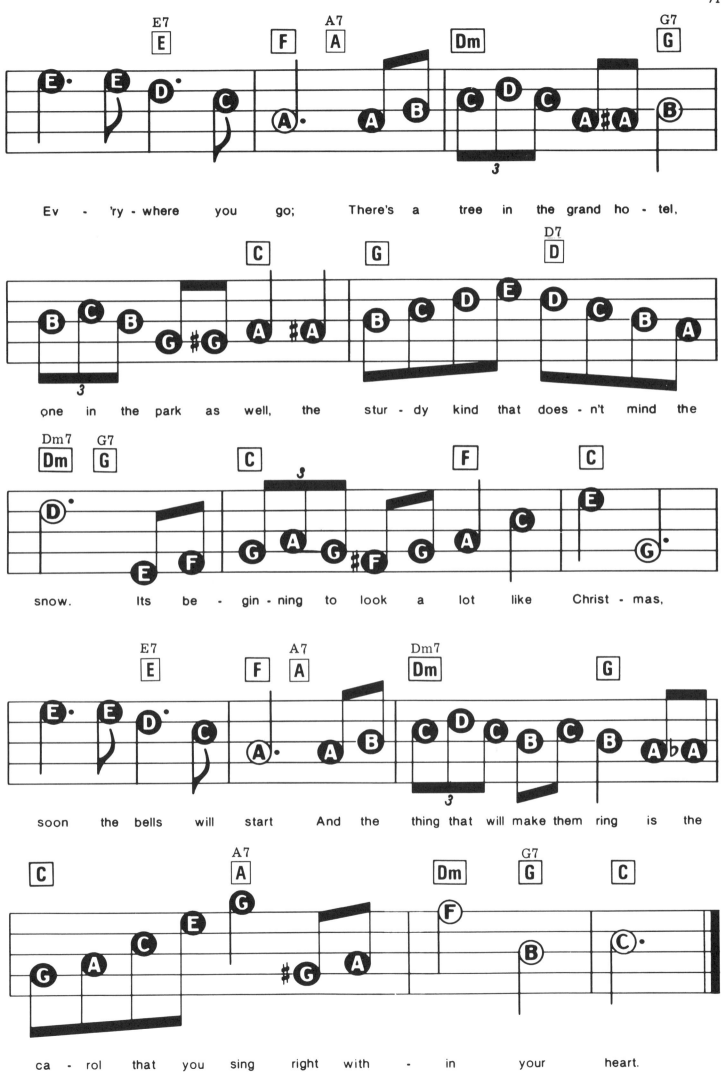

Ev - 'ry - where you go; There's a tree in the grand ho - tel,

one in the park as well, the stur - dy kind that does - n't mind the

snow. Its be - gin - ning to look a lot like Christ - mas,

soon the bells will start And the thing that will make them ring is the

ca - rol that you sing right with - in your heart.

I've Got My Love to Keep Me Warm

from the 20th Century Fox Motion Picture ON THE AVENUE

Registration 4
Rhythm: Fox Trot or Swing

Words and Music by
Irving Berlin

73

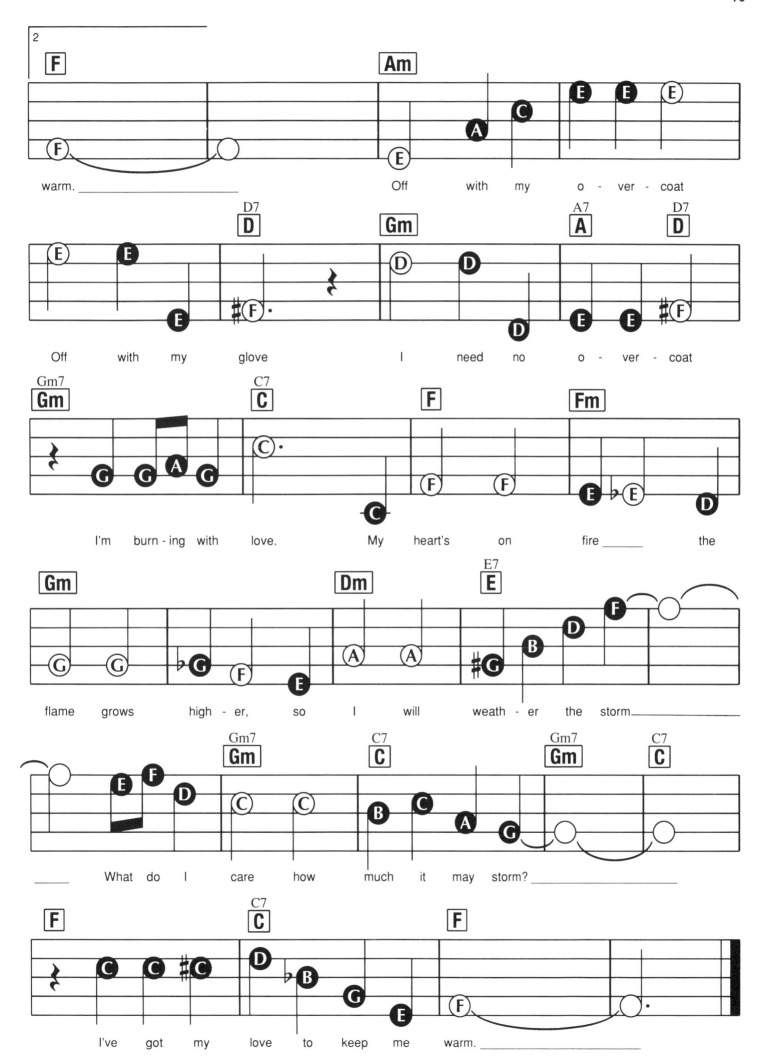

It Won't Seem Like Christmas
(Without You)

Registration 3
Rhythm: Waltz

Words and Music by
J.A. Balthrop

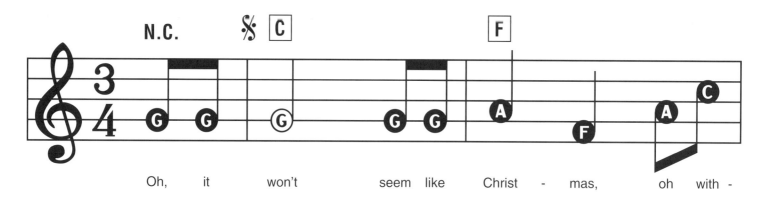

Oh, it won't seem like Christ - mas, oh with -

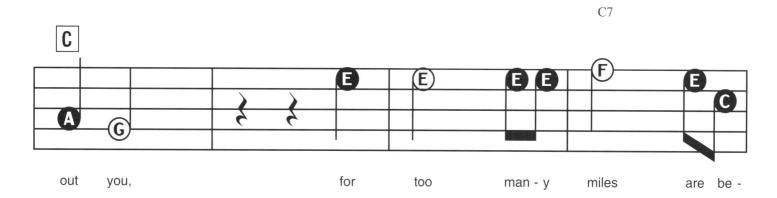

out you, for too man - y miles are be -

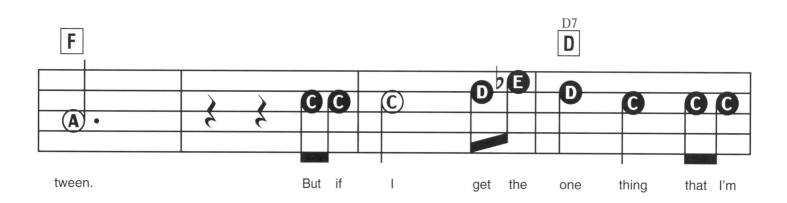

tween. But if I get the one thing that I'm

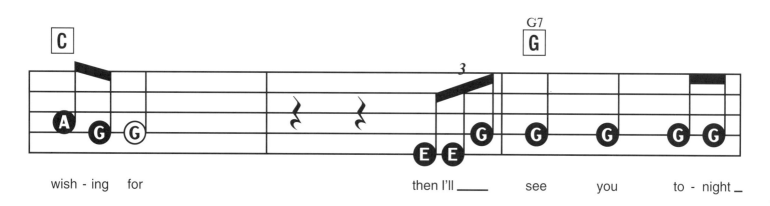

wish - ing for then I'll ____ see you to - night ____

75

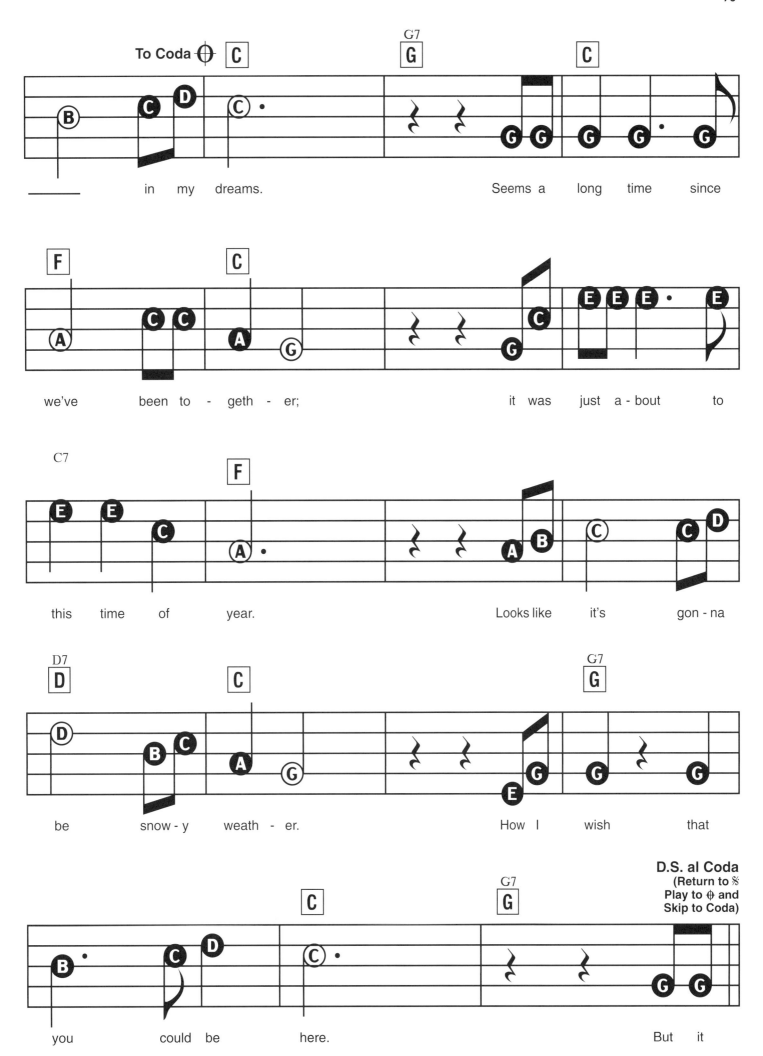

76

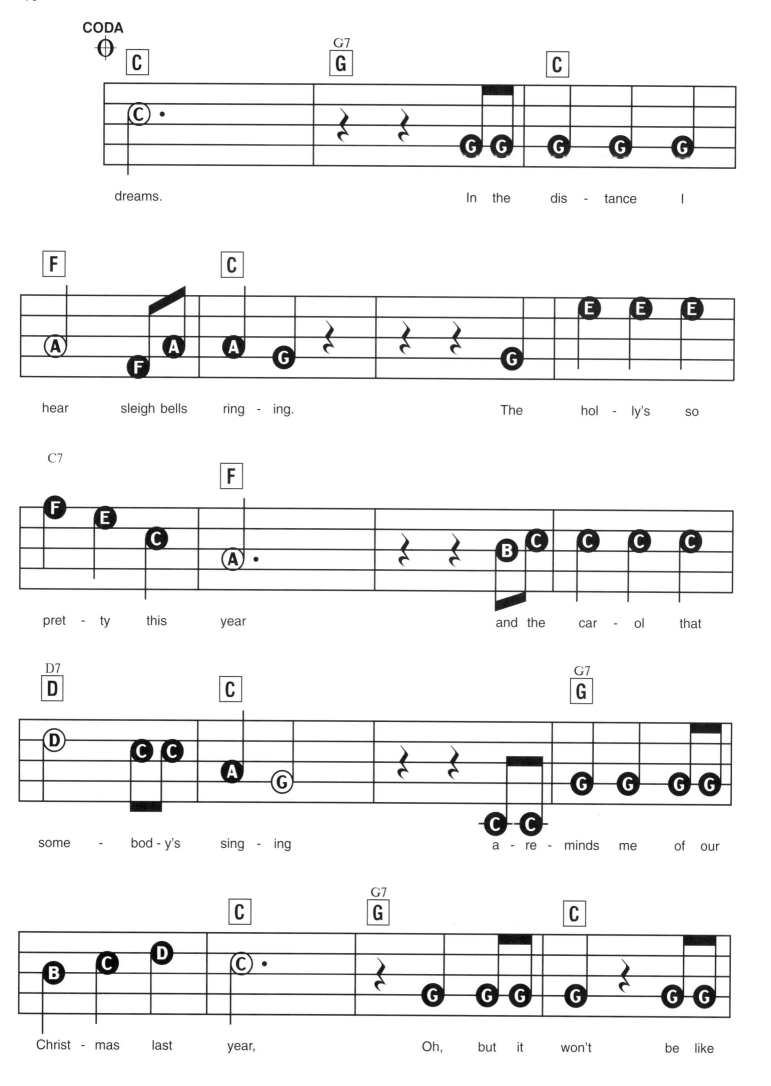

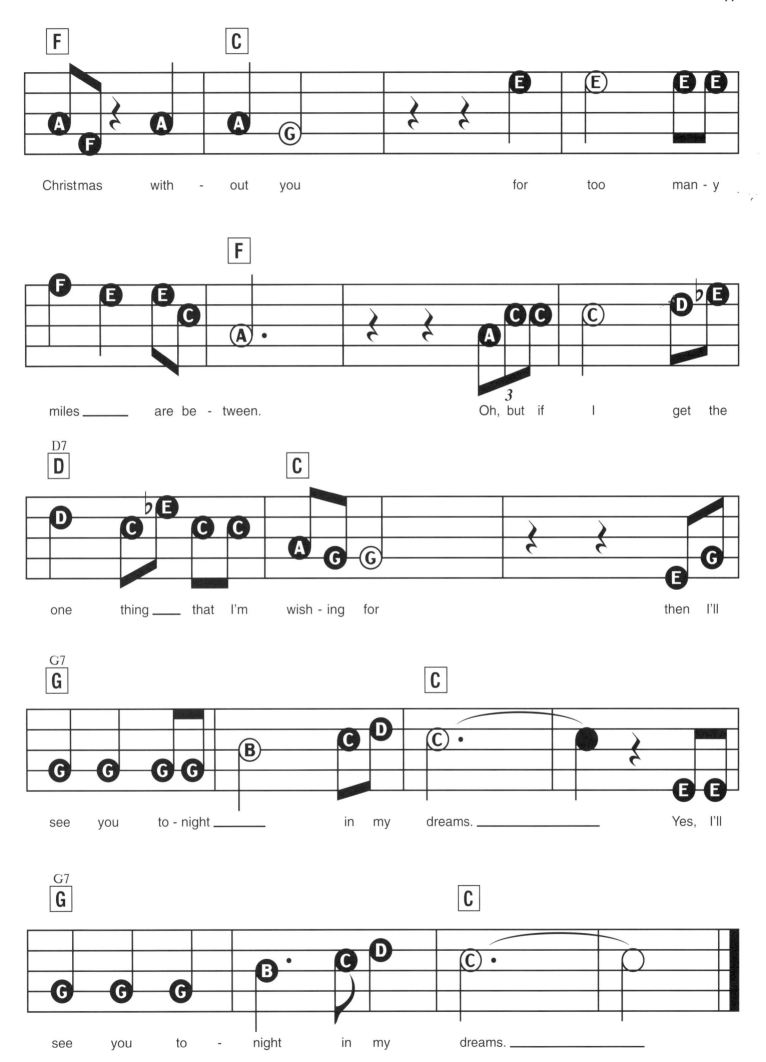

It's Just Another New Year's Eve

Registration 2
Rhythm: Swing

Lyric by Marty Panzer
Music by Barry Manilow

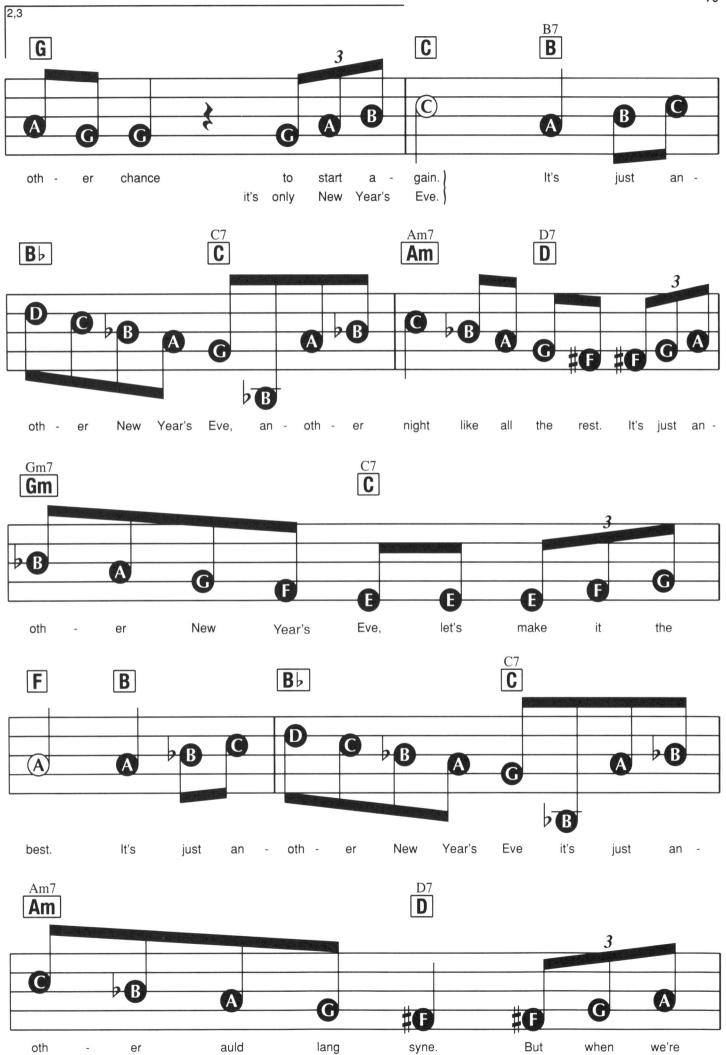

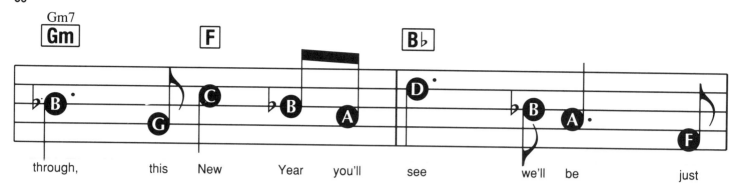

through,   this   New   Year   you'll   see   we'll   be   just

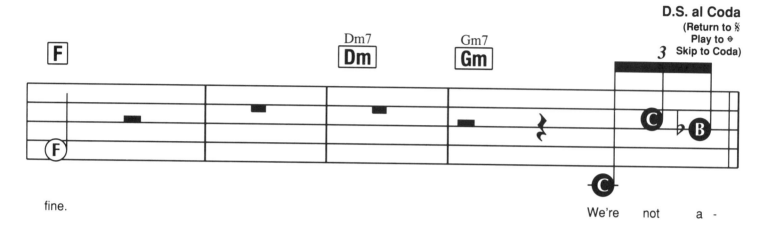

fine.   We're   not   a -

CODA

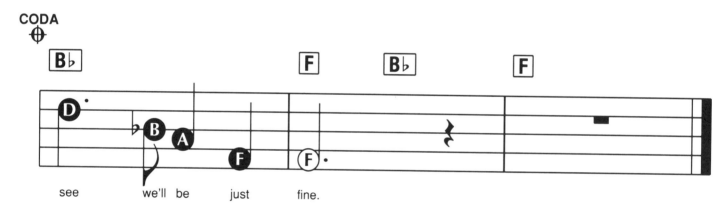

see   we'll be   just   fine.

Additional Lyrics

3. We're not alone,
    We've got the world, you know.
    And it won't let us down,
    Just wait and see.
    And we'll grow old,
    But think how wise we'll grow,
    There's more you know,
    It's only New Year's Eve.

    (Chorus)

Jesus Born on This Day

Registration 2
Rhythm: 8 Beat or Rock

Words and Music by Mariah Carey
and Walter Afanasieff

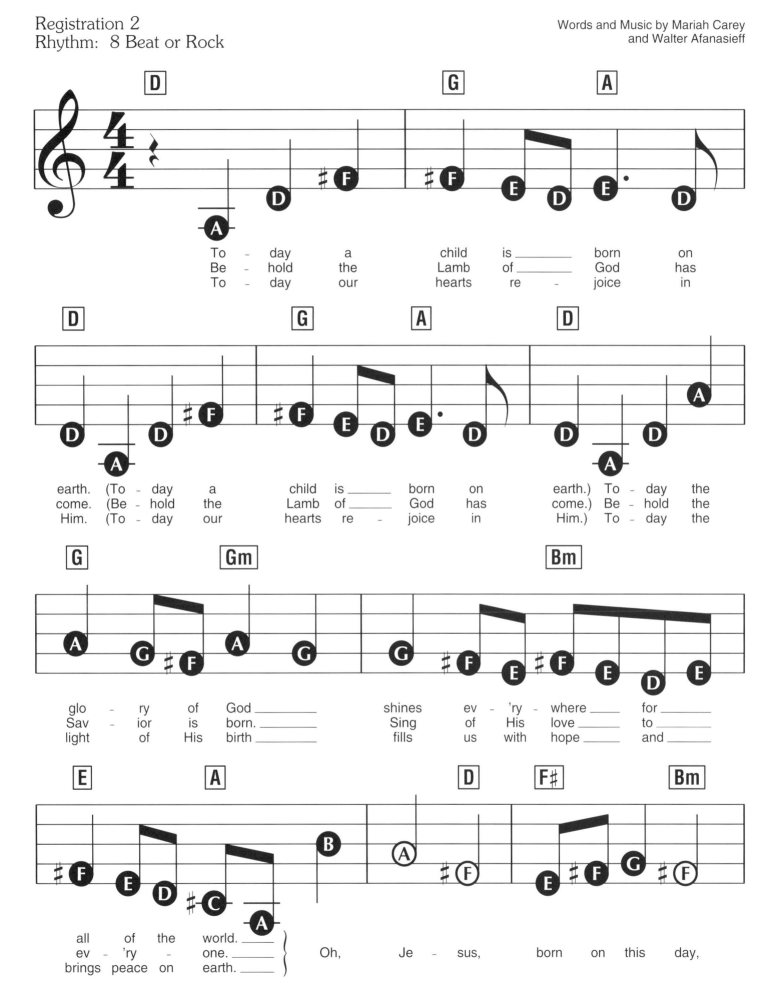

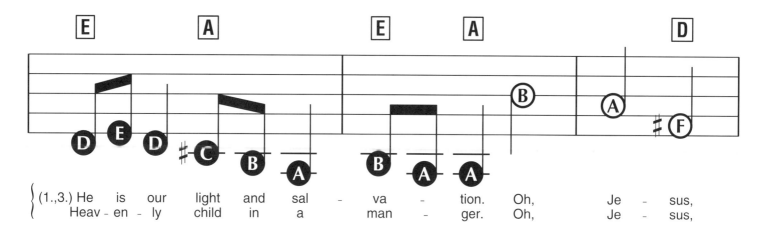

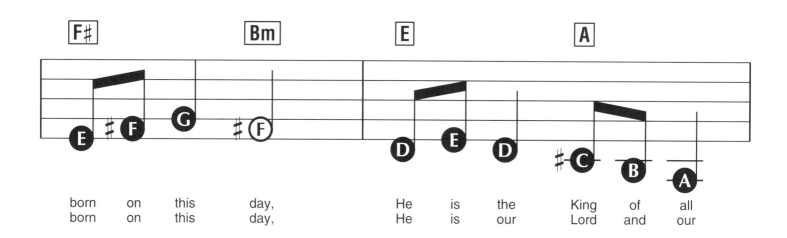

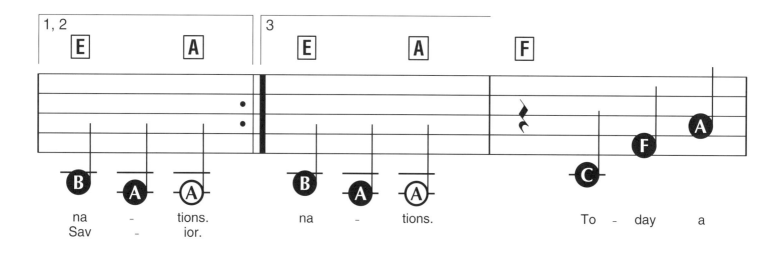

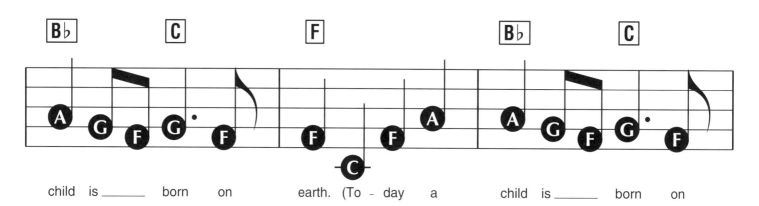

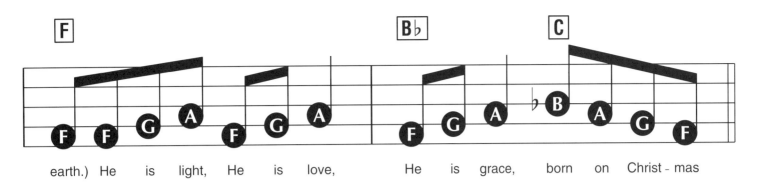

earth.) He is light, He is love, He is grace, born on Christ - mas

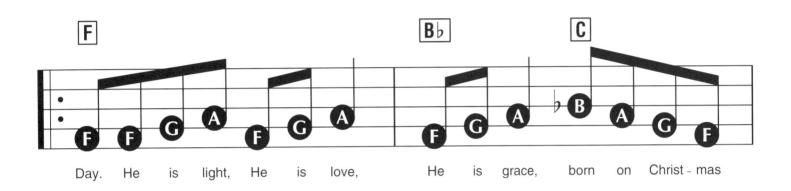

Day. He is light, He is love, He is grace, born on Christ - mas

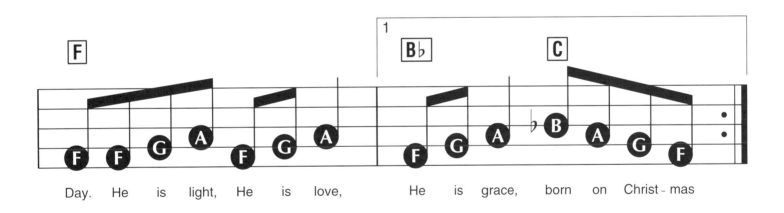

Day. He is light, He is love, He is grace, born on Christ - mas

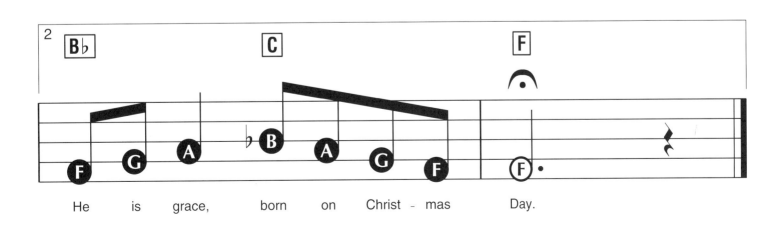

He is grace, born on Christ - mas Day.

Jesus What a Wonderful Child

Registration 8
Rhythm: Swing

Arrangement by Mariah Carey,
Walter Afanasieff and Loris Holland

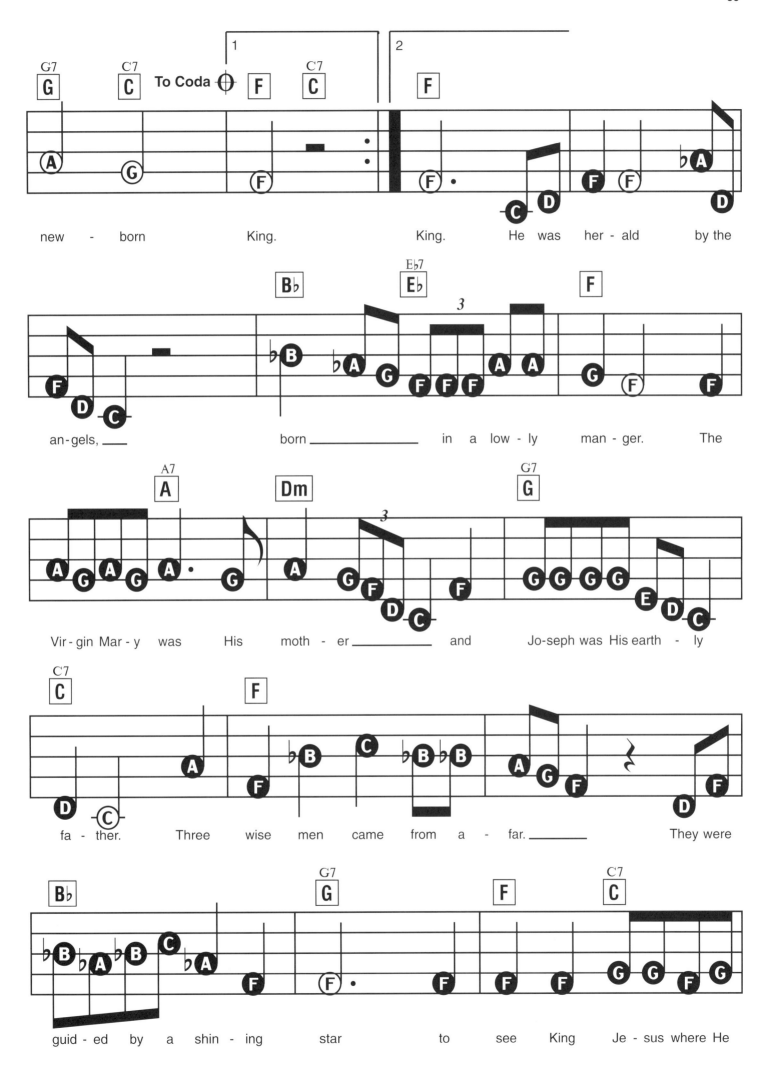

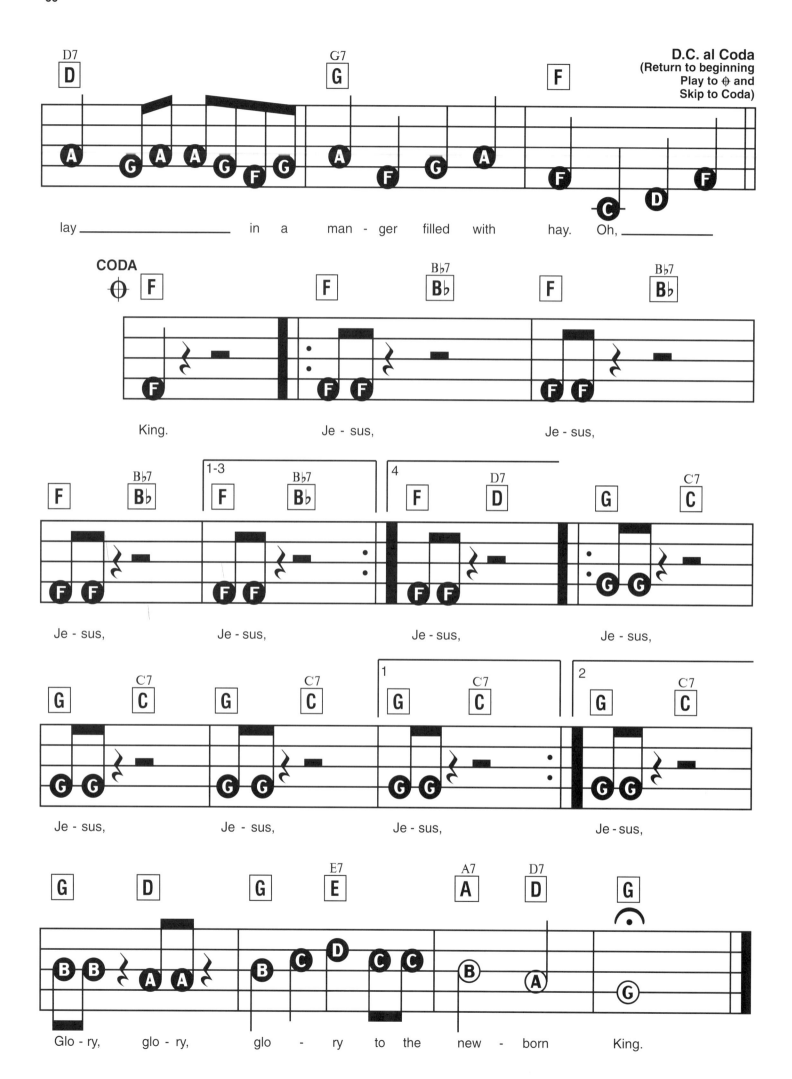

Merry Christmas, Darling

Registration 9
Rhythm: 4/4 Ballad

Words and Music by Richard Carpenter
and Frank Pooler

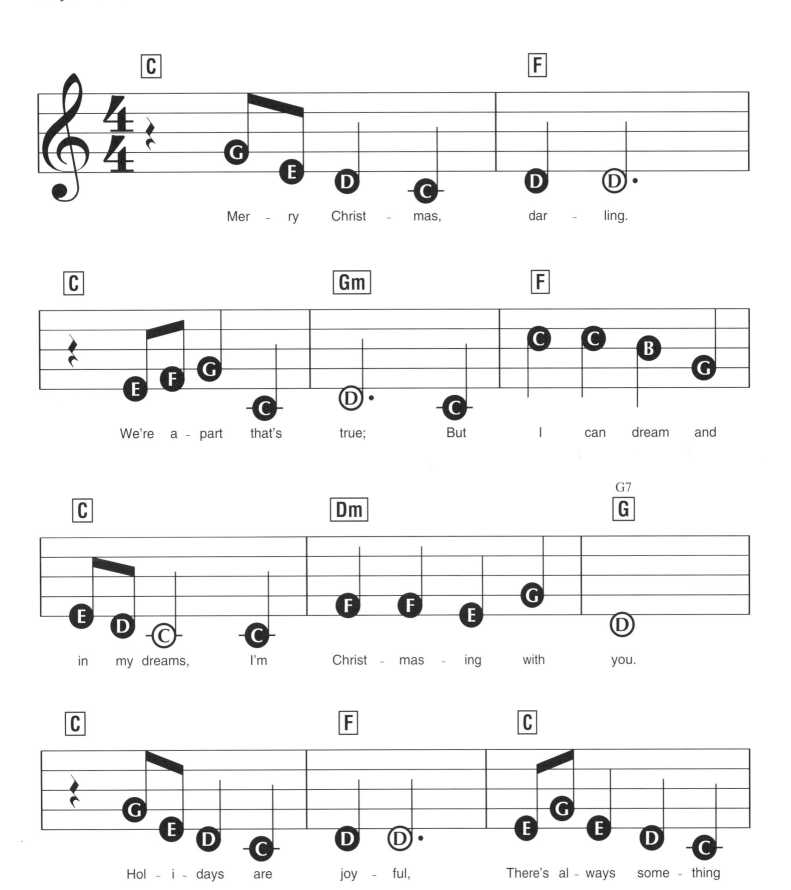

88

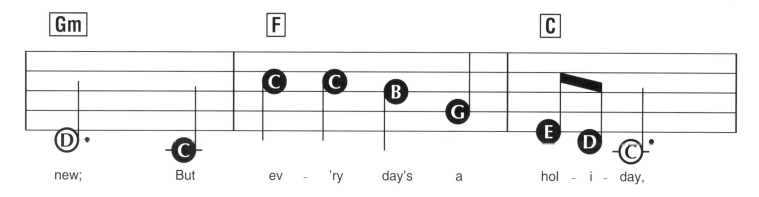

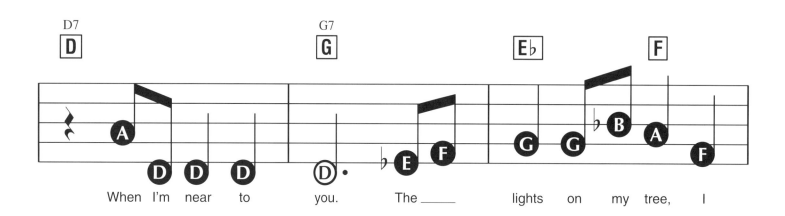

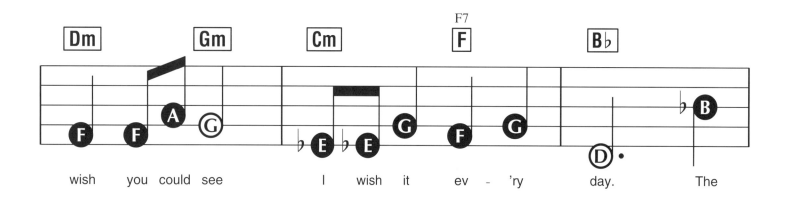

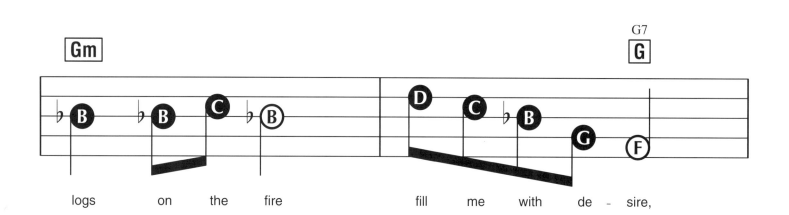

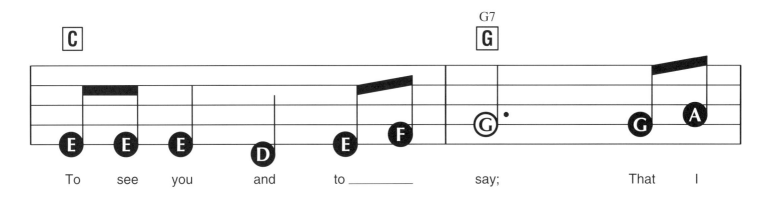

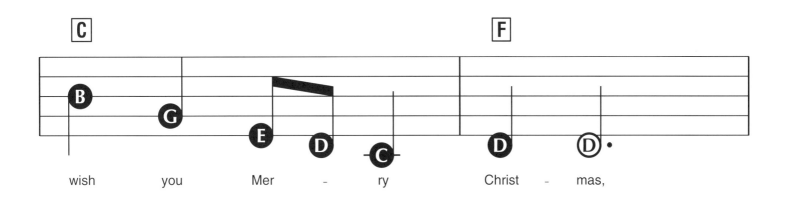

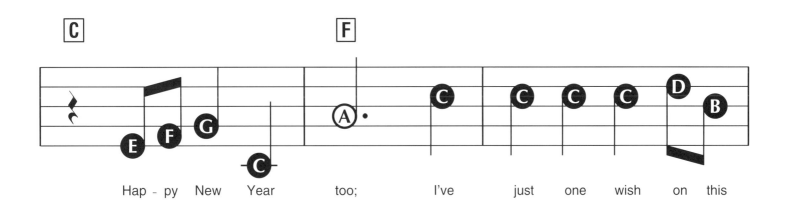

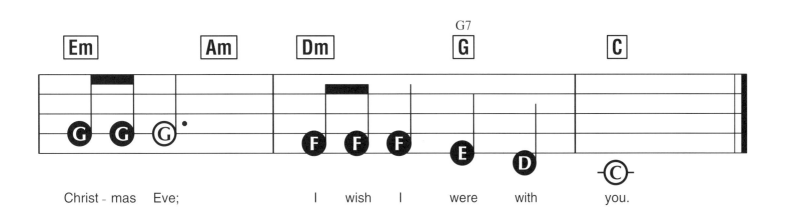

Little Saint Nick

Registration 7
Rhythm: Shuffle or Swing

Words and Music by Brian Wilson
and Mike Love

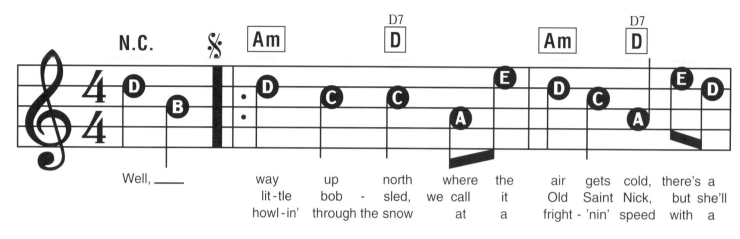

Well, ____ way up north where the air gets cold, there's a
lit-tle bob-sled, we call it Old Saint Nick, but she'll
howl-in' through the snow at a fright-'nin' speed with a

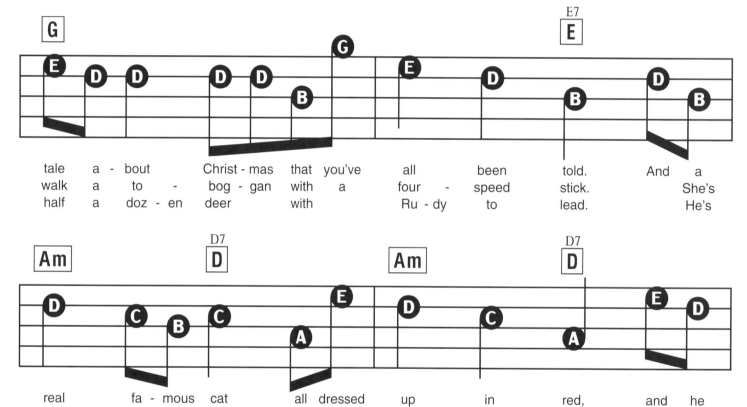

tale a-bout Christ-mas that you've all been told. And a
walk a to-bog-gan with a four-speed stick. She's
half a doz-en deer with Ru-dy to lead. He's

real fa-mous cat all dressed up in red, and he
can-dy ap-ple red with a ski for a wheel, and when
got-ta wear his gog-gles 'cause the snow real-ly flies, and he's

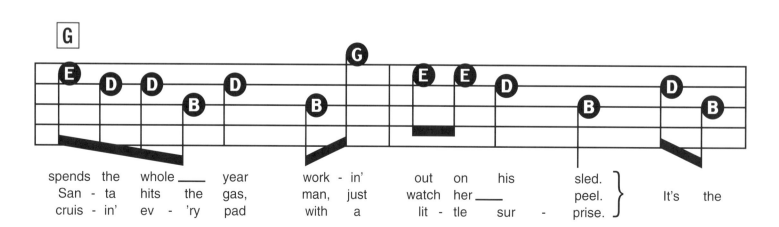

spends the whole ____ year work-in' out on his sled.
San-ta hits the gas, man, just watch her ____ peel. } It's the
cruis-in' ev-'ry pad with a lit-tle sur-prise.

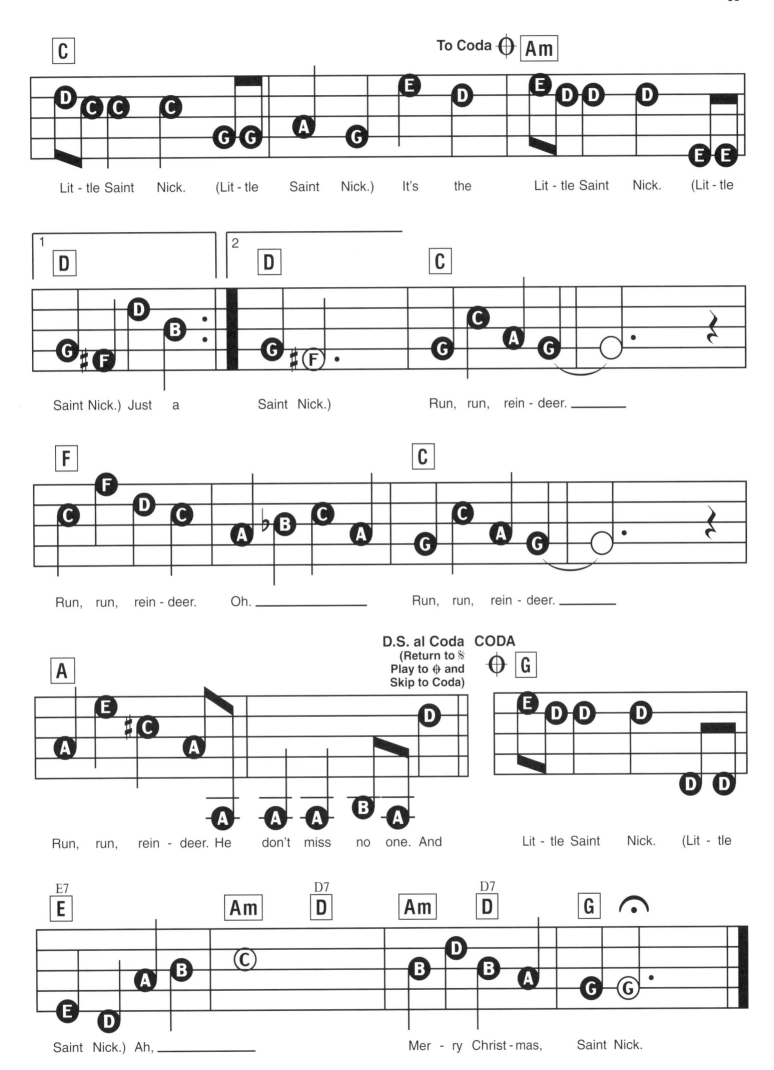

Mary's Little Boy

Registration 3
Rhythm: Calypso or Latin

Words and Music by Massie Patterson
and Sammy Heyward

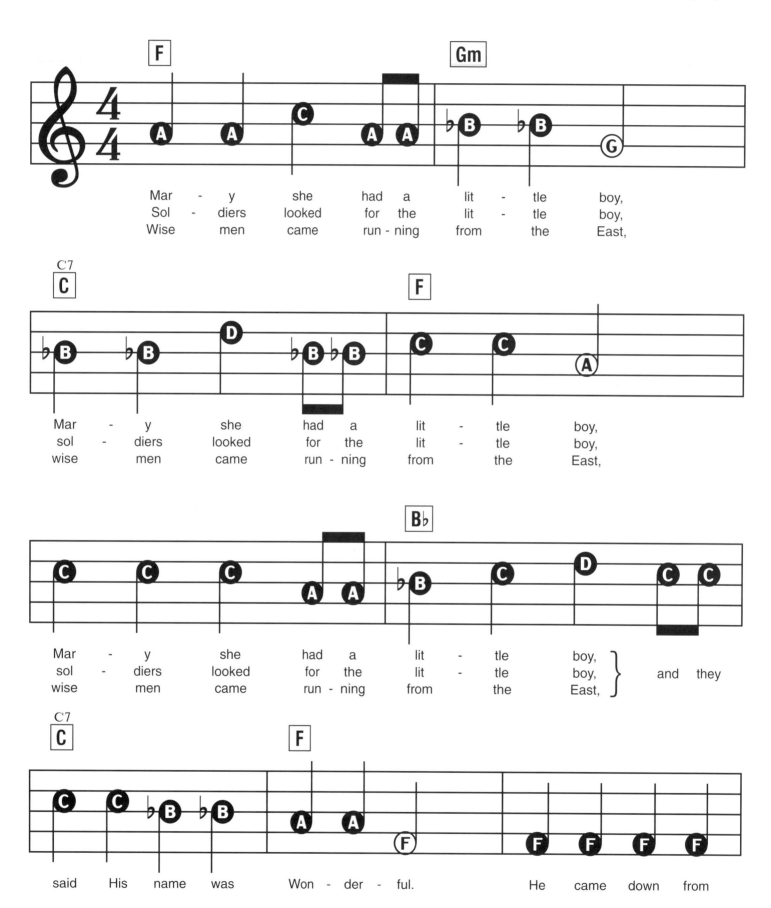

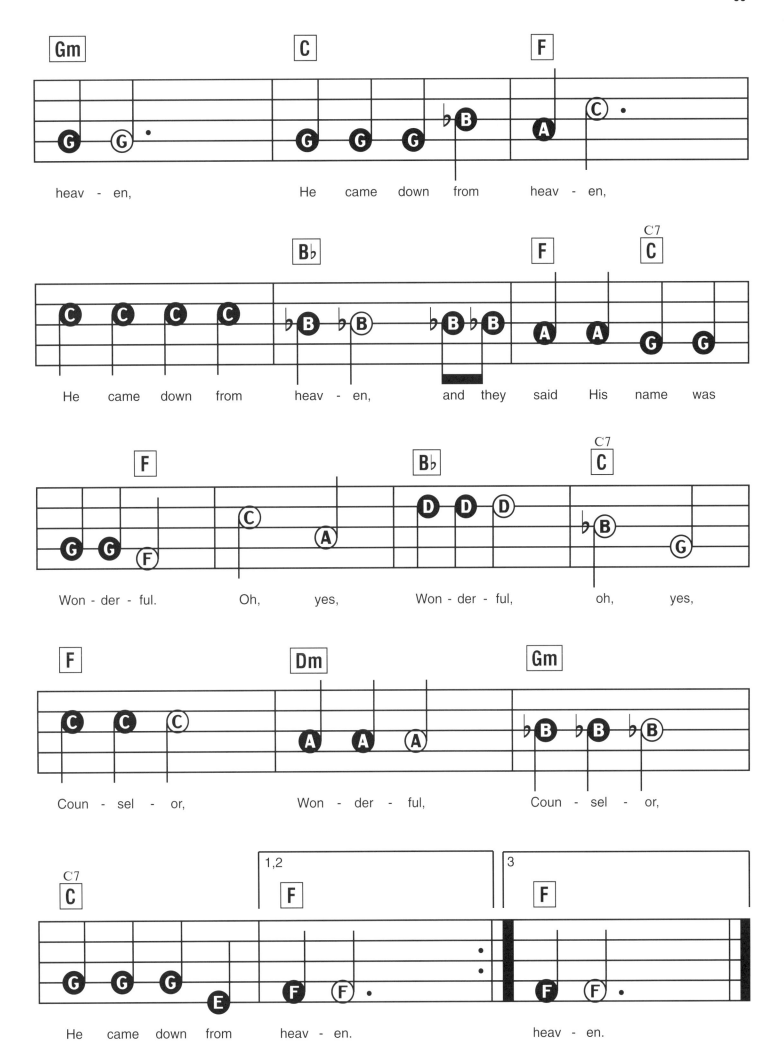

Merry Christmas from the Family

Registration 7
Rhythm: Fox Trot or Swing

Words and Music by
Robert Earl Keen

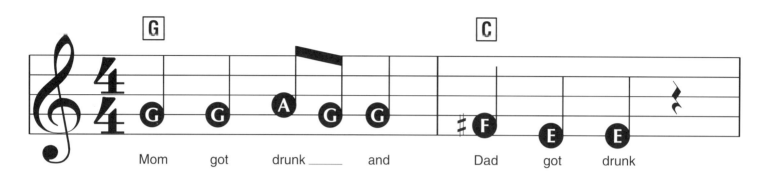

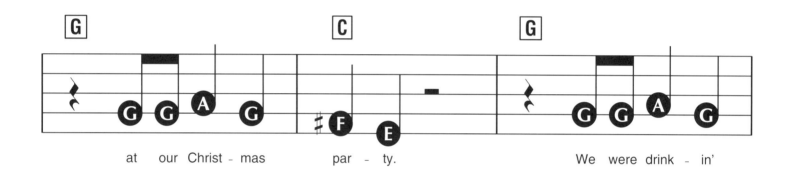

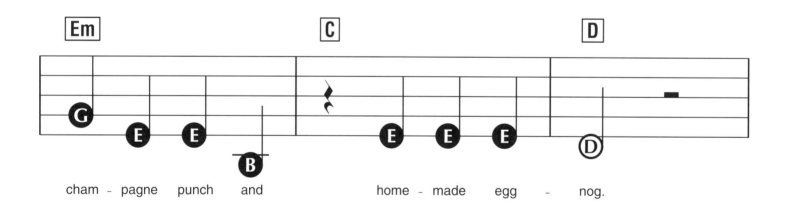

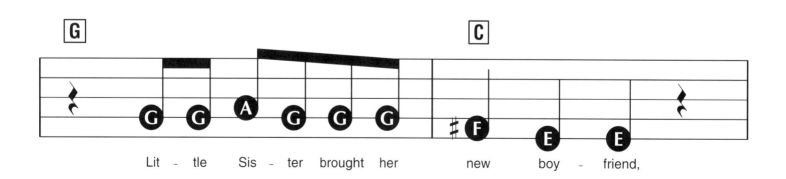

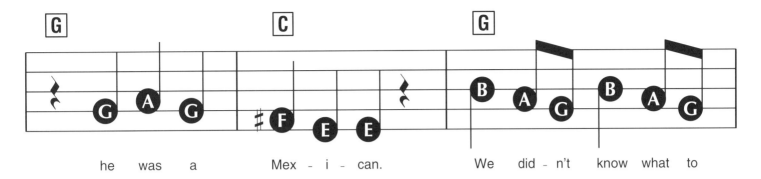

he was a Mex – i – can. We did – n't know what to

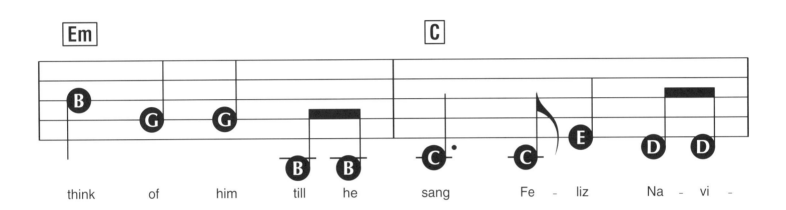

think of him till he sang Fe – liz Na – vi –

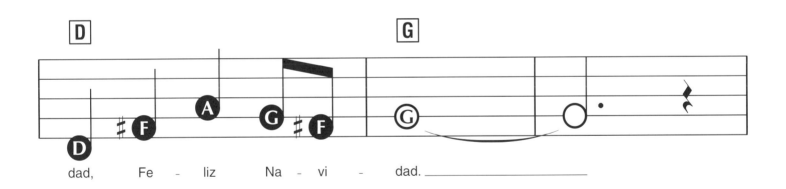

dad, Fe – liz Na – vi – dad. _____

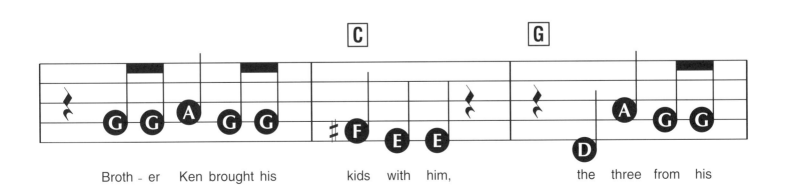

Broth – er Ken brought his kids with him, the three from his

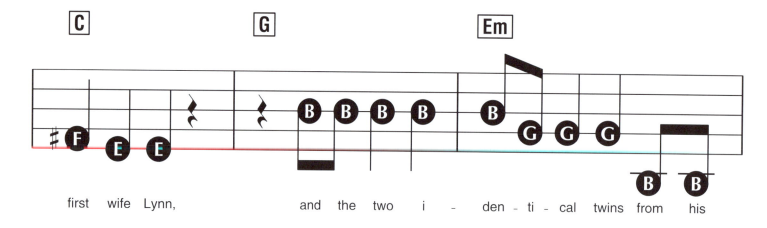

first wife Lynn, and the two i – den – ti – cal twins from his

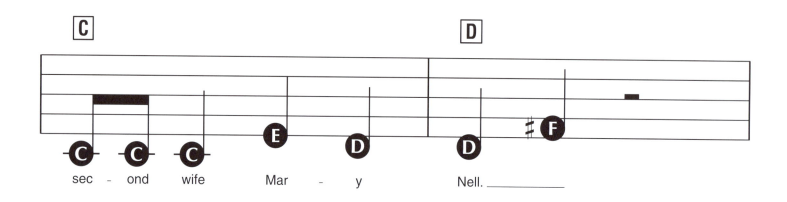

sec – ond wife Mar – y Nell. _____

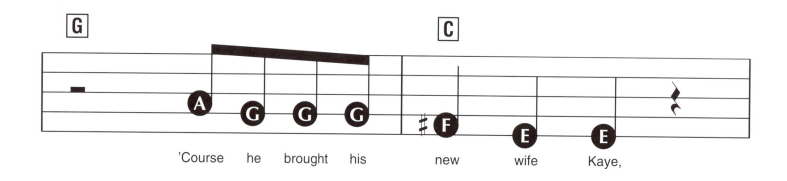

'Course he brought his new wife Kaye,

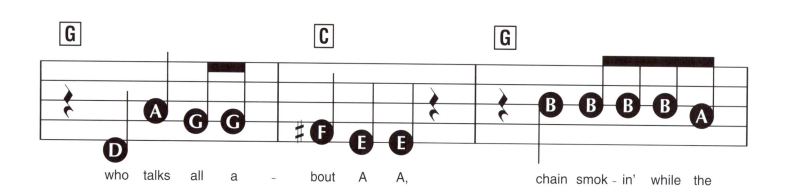

who talks all a – bout A A, chain smok – in' while the

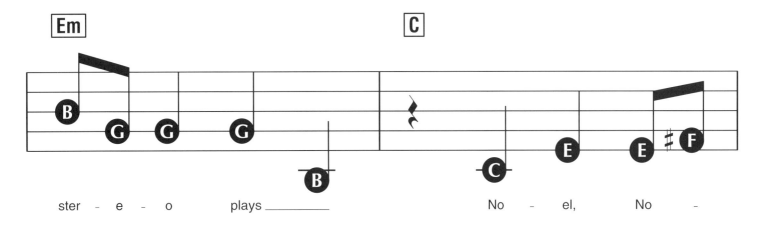

ster - e - o plays _____ No - el, No -

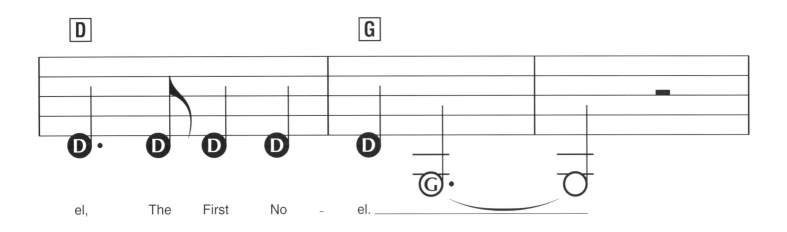

el, The First No - el. _____

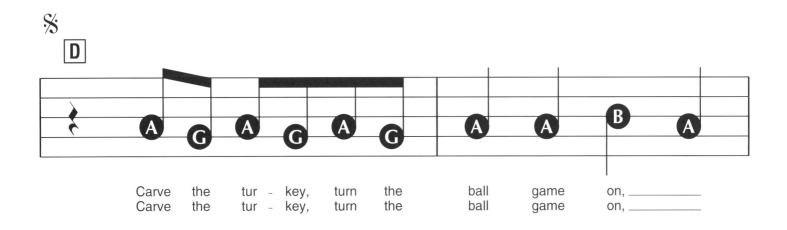

Carve the tur - key, turn the ball game on, _____
Carve the tur - key, turn the ball game on, _____

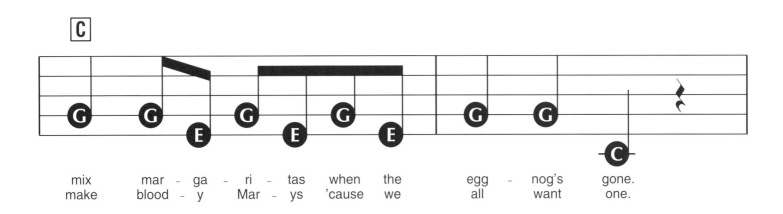

mix mar - ga - ri - tas when the egg - nog's gone.
make blood - y Mar - ys 'cause we all want one.

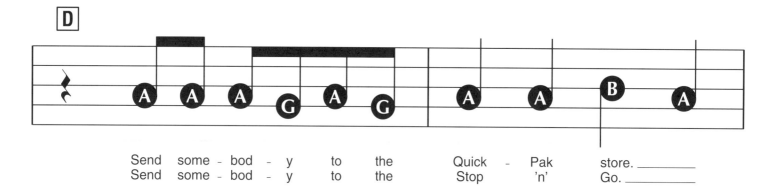

D

Send some-bod – y to the Quick - Pak store. _____
Send some-bod – y to the Stop 'n' Go. _____

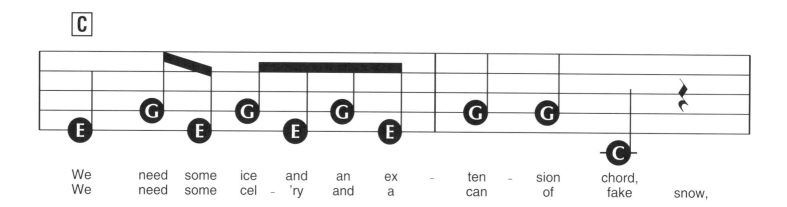

C

We need some ice and an ex – ten – sion chord,
We need some cel – 'ry and a can of fake snow,

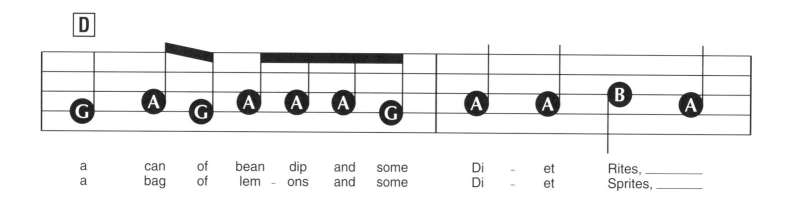

D

a can of bean dip and some Di – et Rites, _____
a bag of lem – ons and some Di – et Sprites, _____

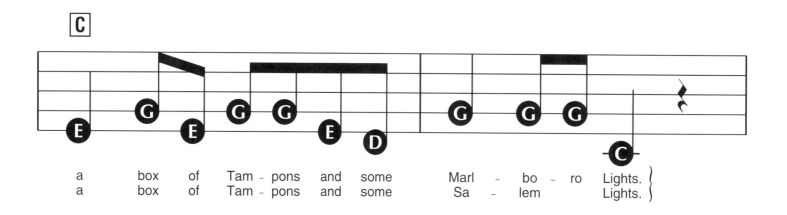

C

a box of Tam – pons and some Marl – bo – ro Lights. }
a box of Tam – pons and some Sa – lem Lights. }

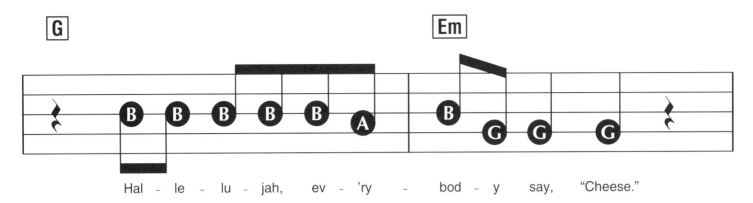

Hal - le - lu - jah, ev - 'ry - bod - y say, "Cheese."

To Coda ⊕

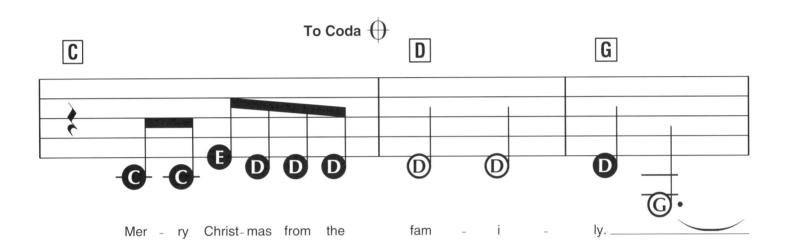

Mer - ry Christ-mas from the fam - i - ly. _____

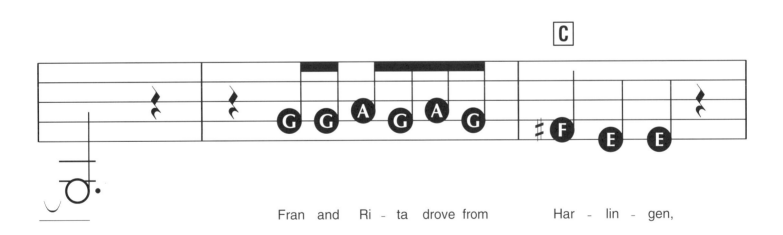

Fran and Ri - ta drove from Har - lin - gen,

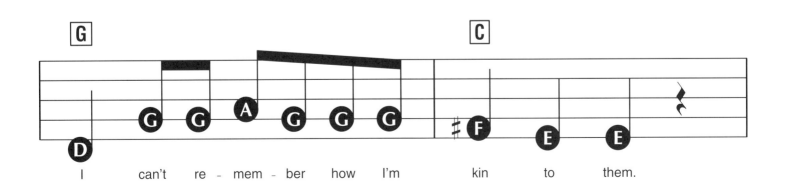

I can't re - mem - ber how I'm kin to them.

100

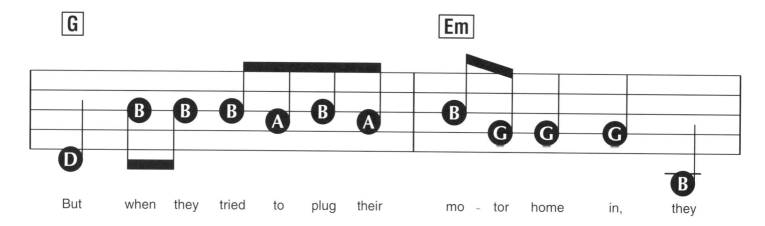

But when they tried to plug their motor home in, they

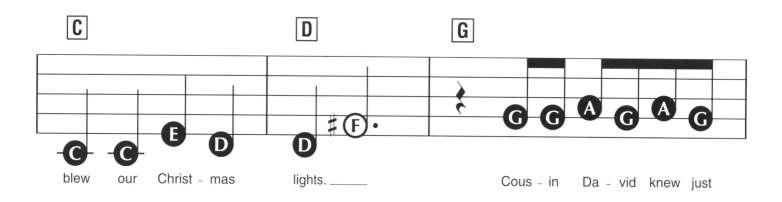

blew our Christ - mas lights. _____ Cous - in Da - vid knew just

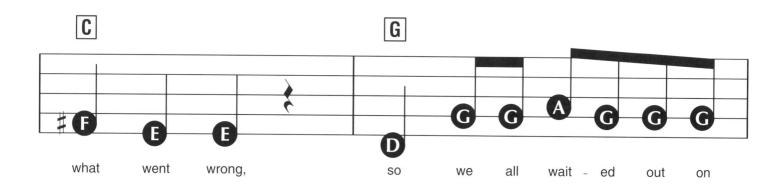

what went wrong, so we all wait - ed out on

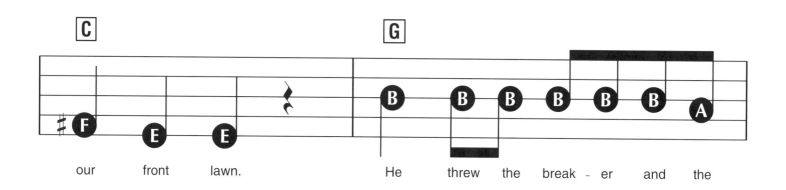

our front lawn. He threw the break - er and the

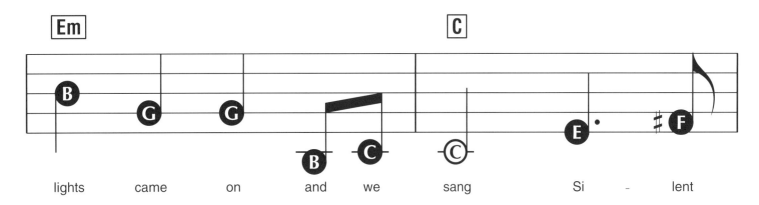

lights   came   on   and   we   sang   Si   -   lent

D.S. al Coda
(Return to %
Play to ⊕ and
Skip to Coda)

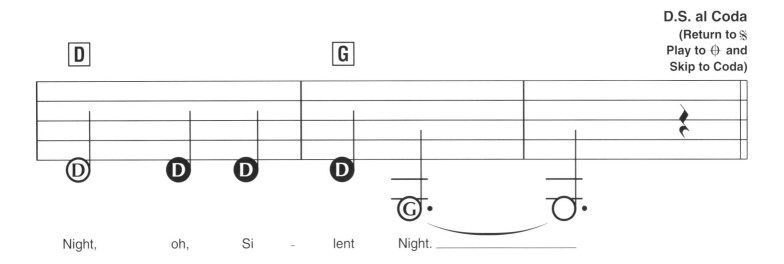

Night,   oh,   Si   -   lent   Night. _____

CODA
⊕

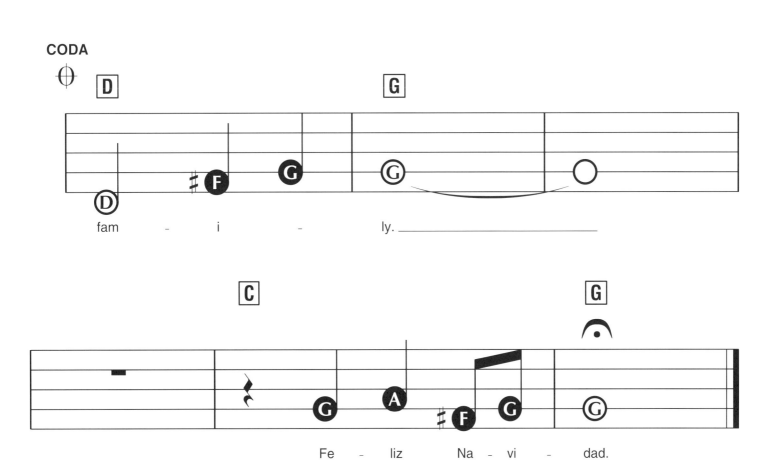

fam   -   i   -   ly. _____

Fe   -   liz   Na   -   vi   -   dad.

Merry, Merry Christmas, Baby

Registration 2
Rhythm: Slow Rock

Words and Music by Margo Sylvia
and Gilbert Lopez

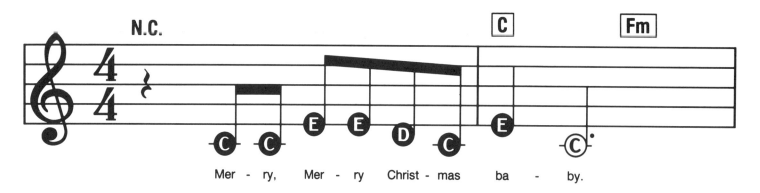

Mer - ry, Mer - ry Christ - mas ba - by.

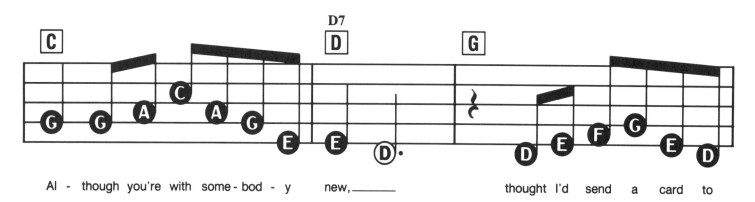

Al - though you're with some - bod - y new,_____ thought I'd send a card to

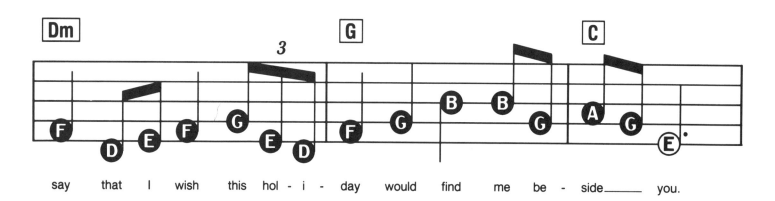

say that I wish this hol - i - day would find me be - side_____ you.

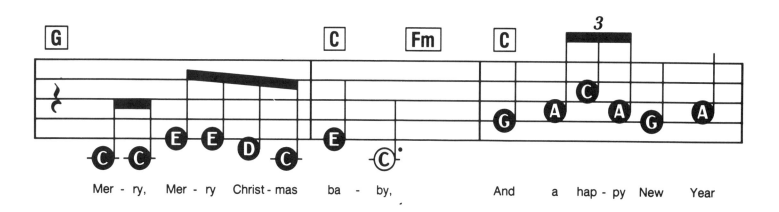

Mer - ry, Mer - ry Christ - mas ba - by, And a hap - py New Year

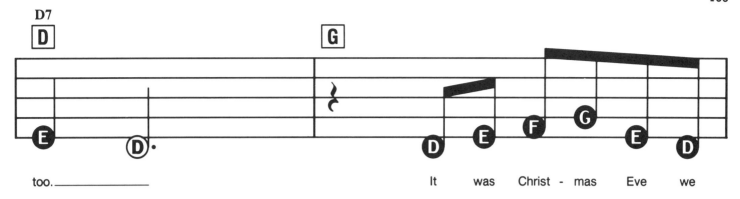

too._____ It was Christ - mas Eve we

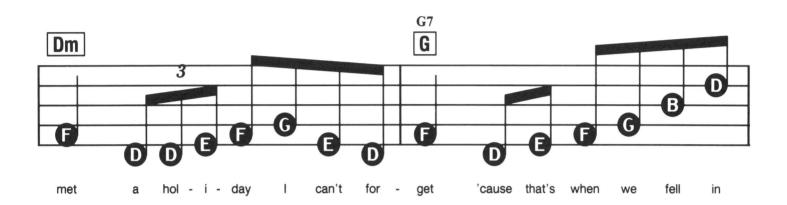

met a hol - i - day I can't for - get 'cause that's when we fell in

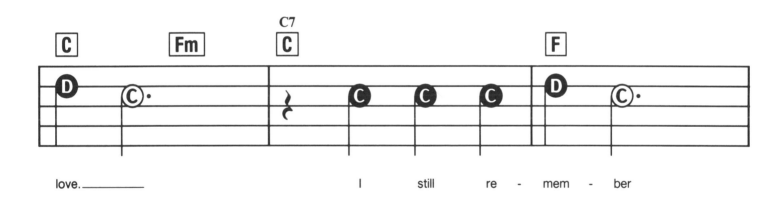

love._____ I still re - mem - ber

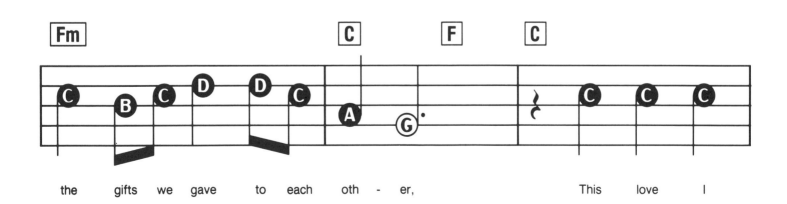

the gifts we gave to each oth - er, This love I

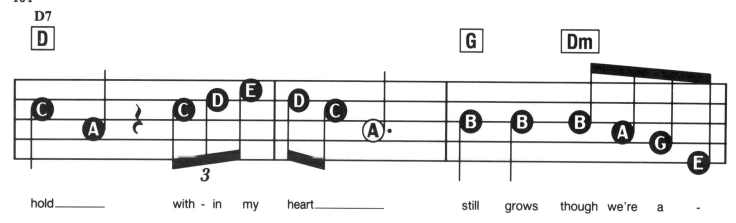

hold_____ with - in my heart_____ still grows though we're a -

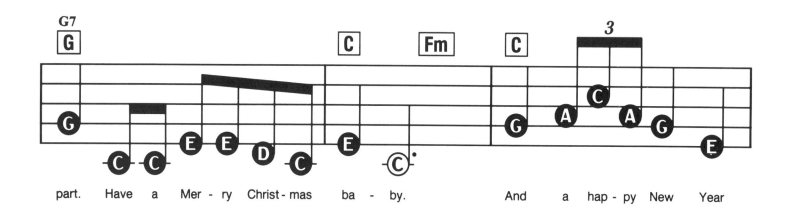

part. Have a Mer - ry Christ - mas ba - by. And a hap - py New Year

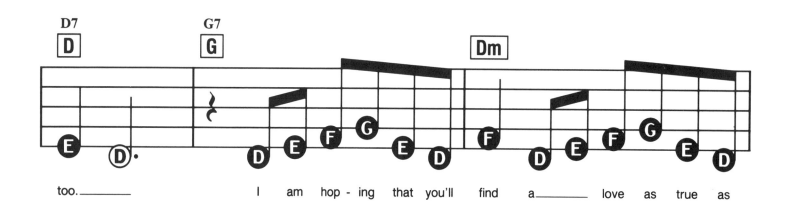

too._____ I am hop - ing that you'll find a_____ love as true as

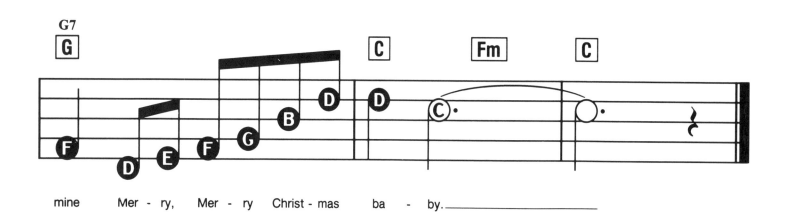

mine Mer - ry, Mer - ry Christ - mas ba - by._____

Silver Bells
from the Paramount Picture THE LEMON DROP KID

Registration 7
Rhythm: Waltz

Words and Music by Jay Livingston
and Ray Evans

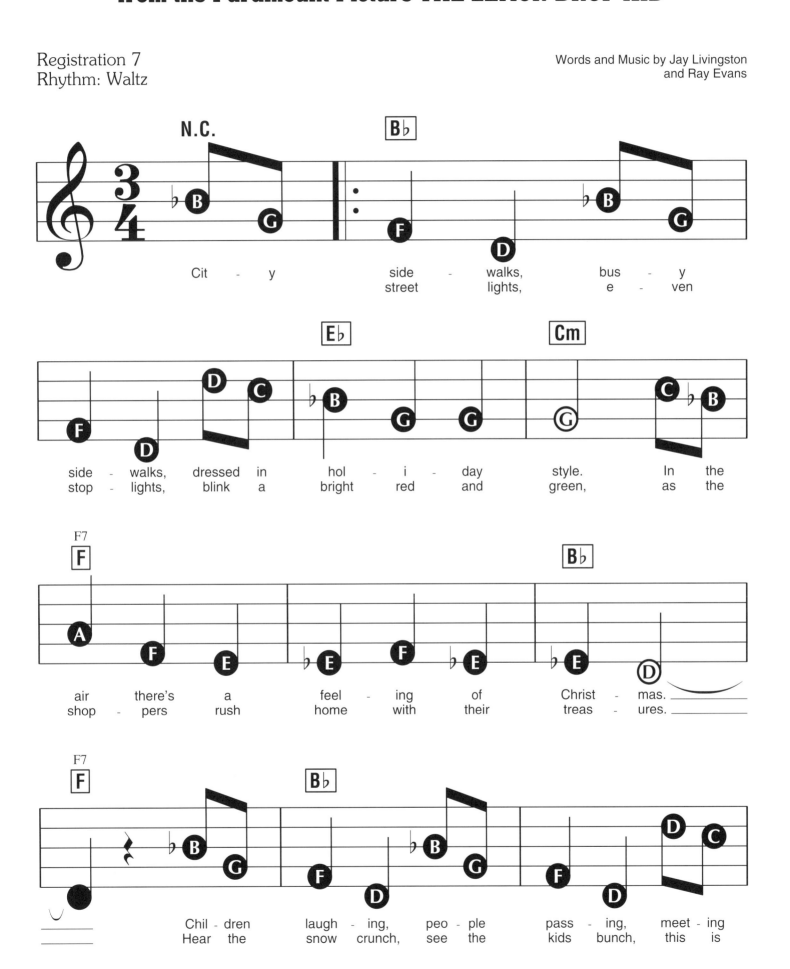

106

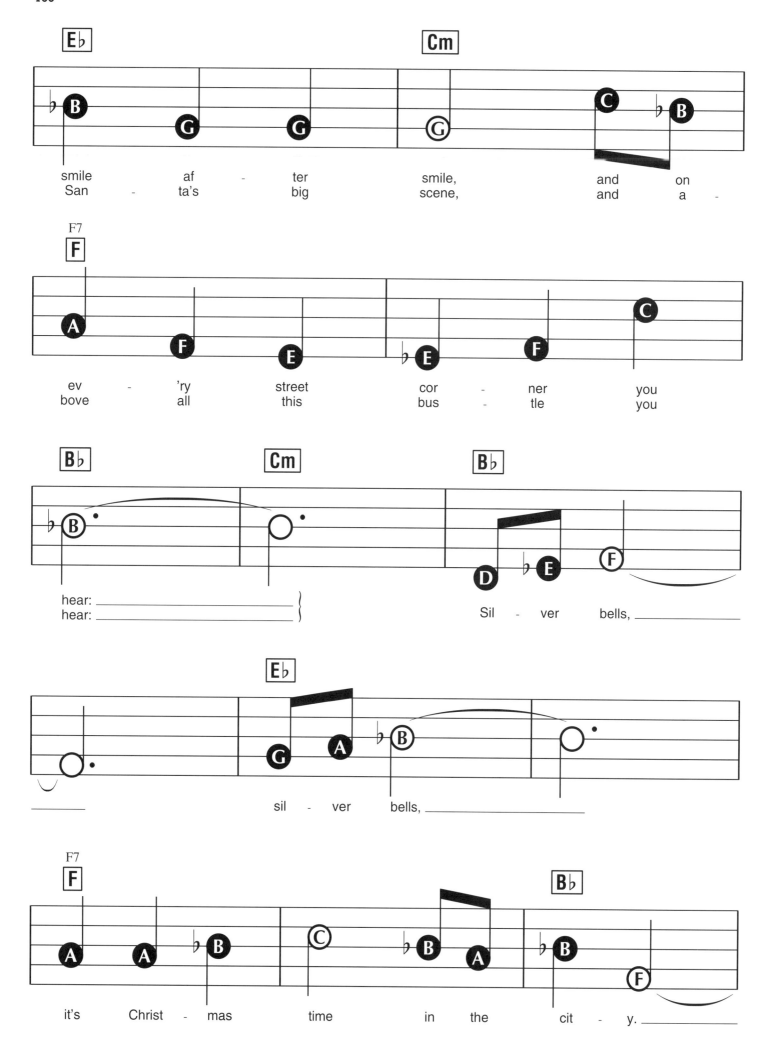

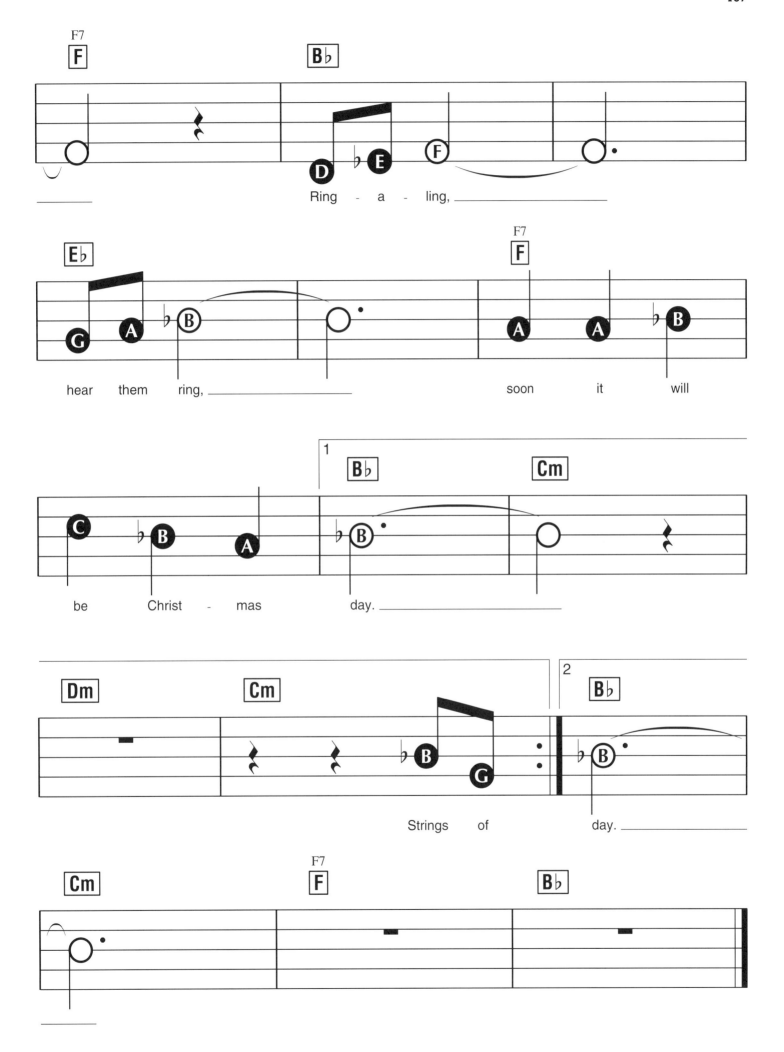

The Most Wonderful Time of the Year

Registration 4
Rhythm: Jazz Waltz or Waltz

Words and Music by Eddie Pola
and George Wyle

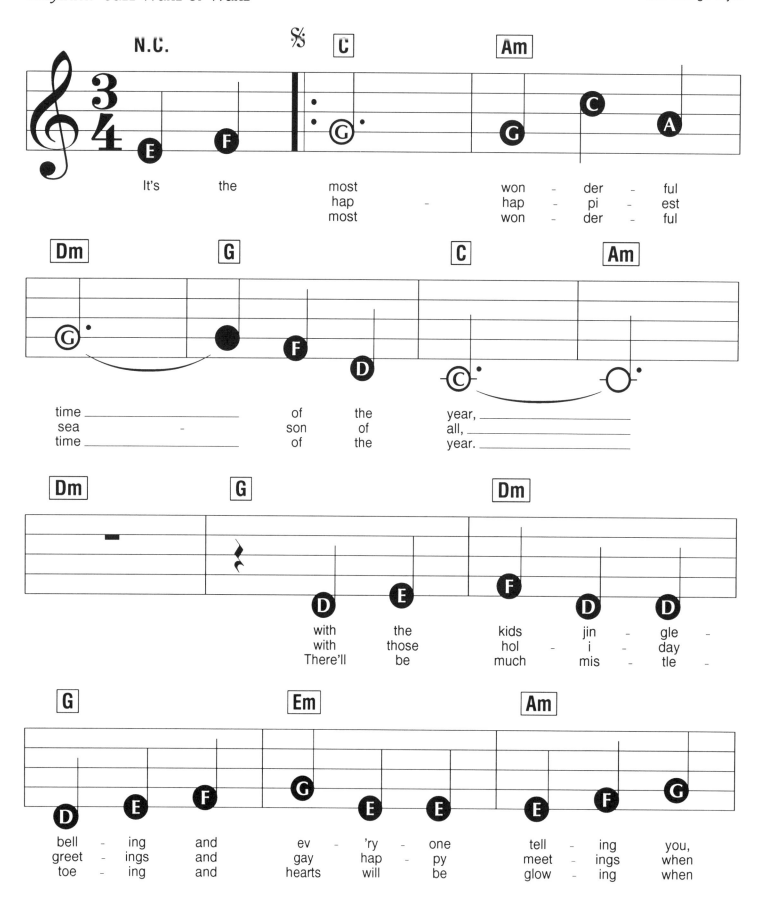

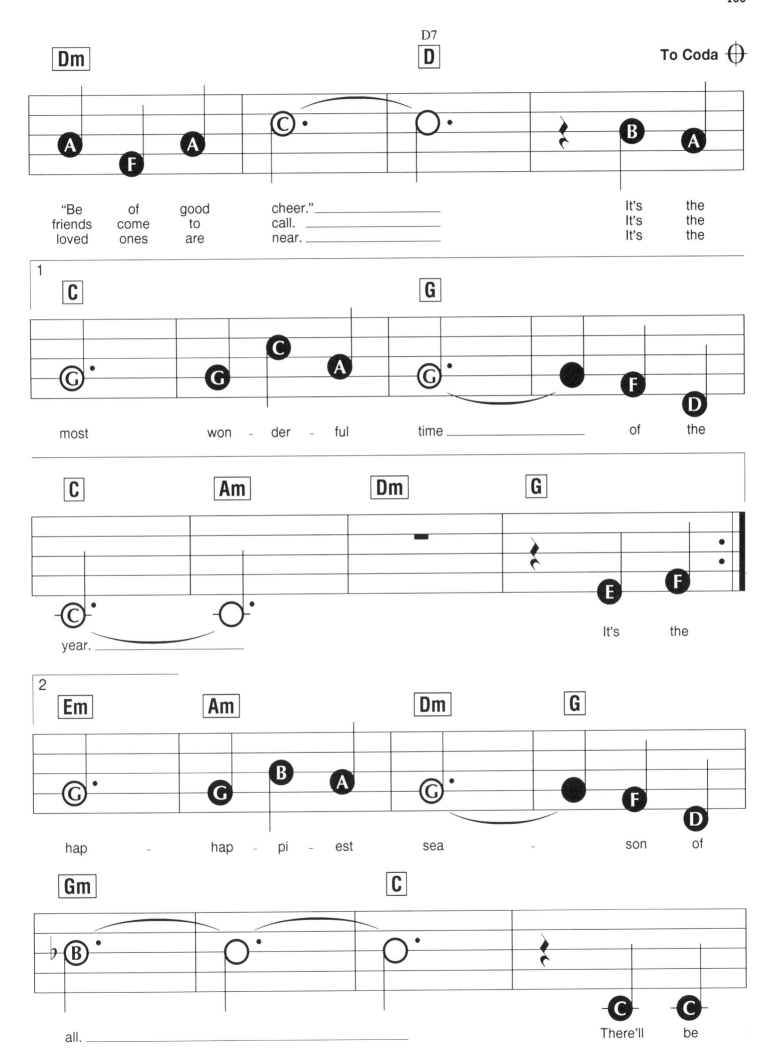

110

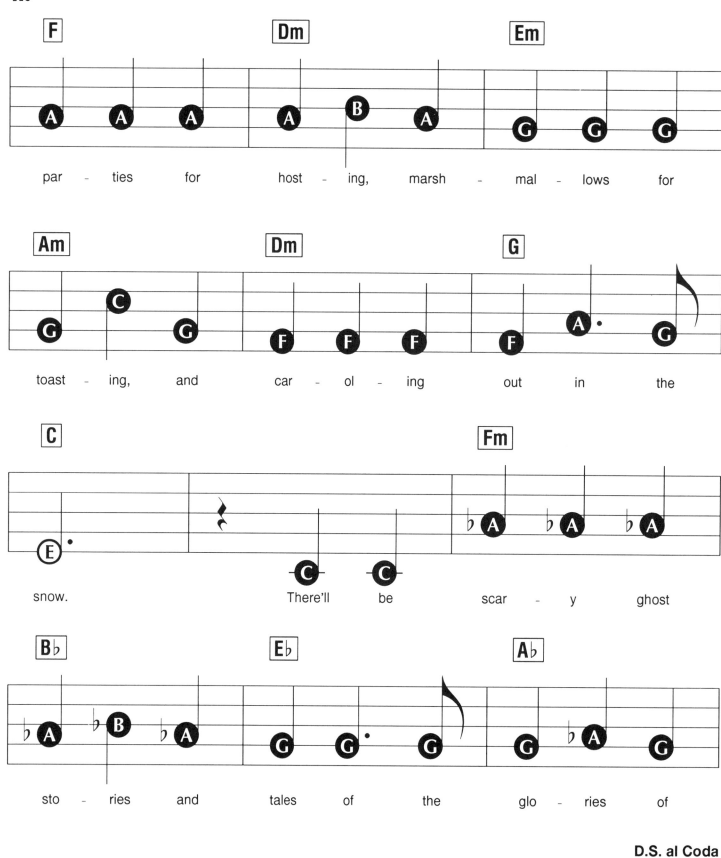

D.S. al Coda
(Return to 𝄋
Play to ⊕ and
Skip to Coda)

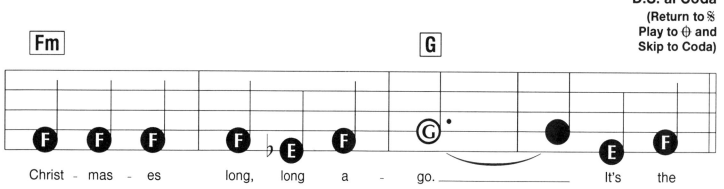

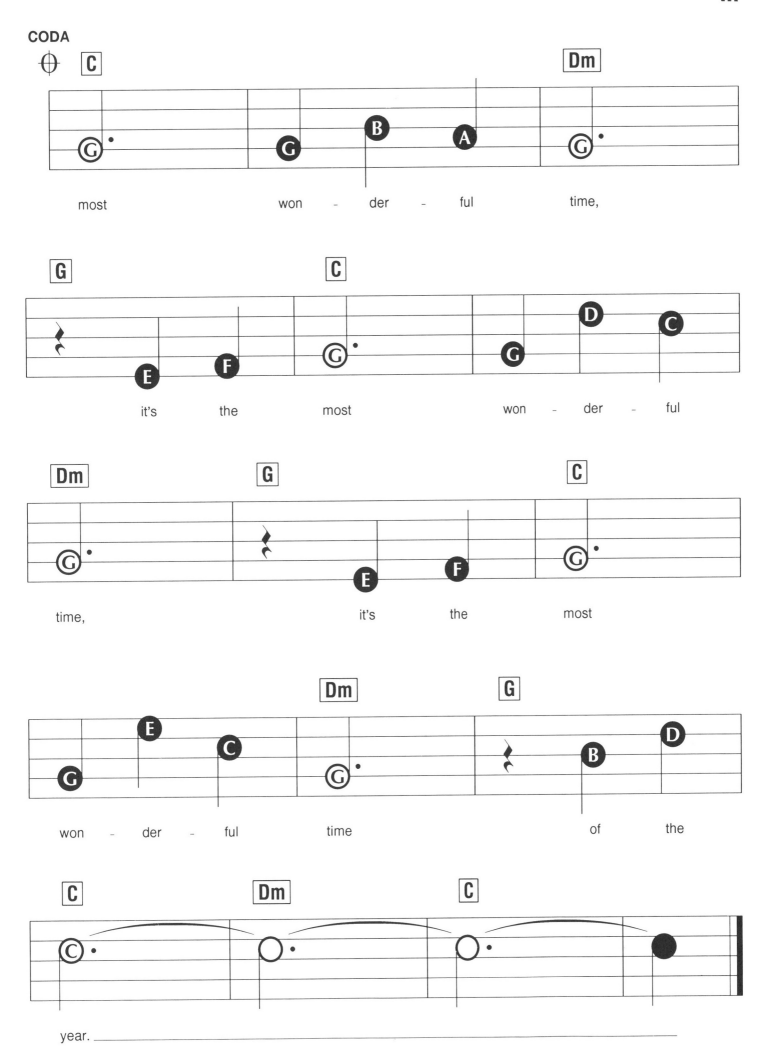

Poor Little Jesus

Registration 1
Rhythm: Fox Trot

Arranged by Ronnie Gilbert, Lee Hays,
Fred Hellerman and Pete Seeger

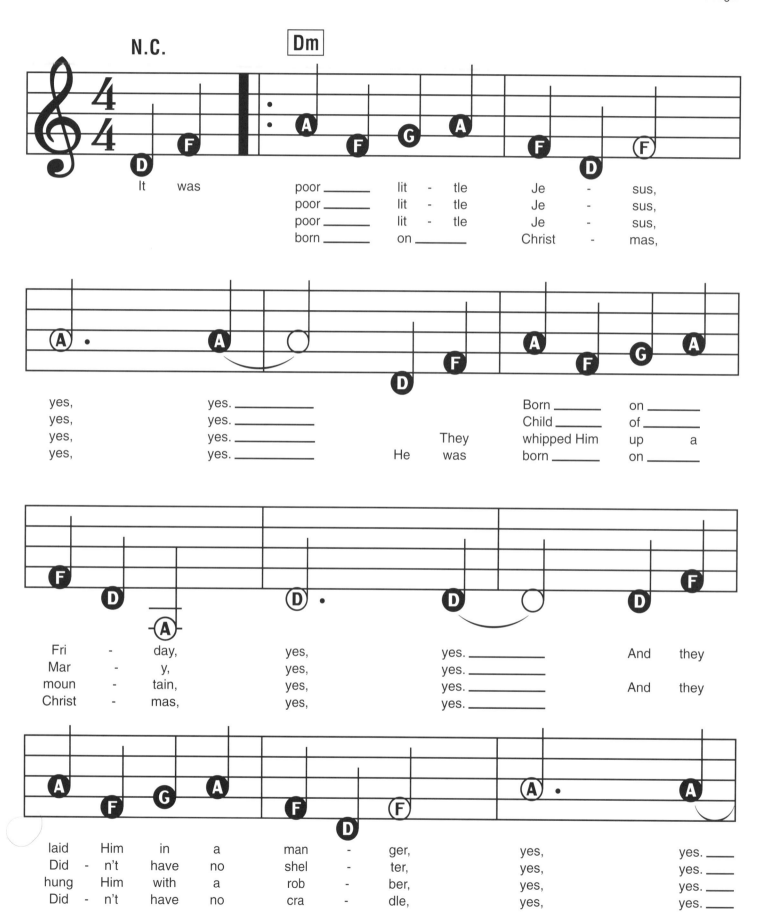

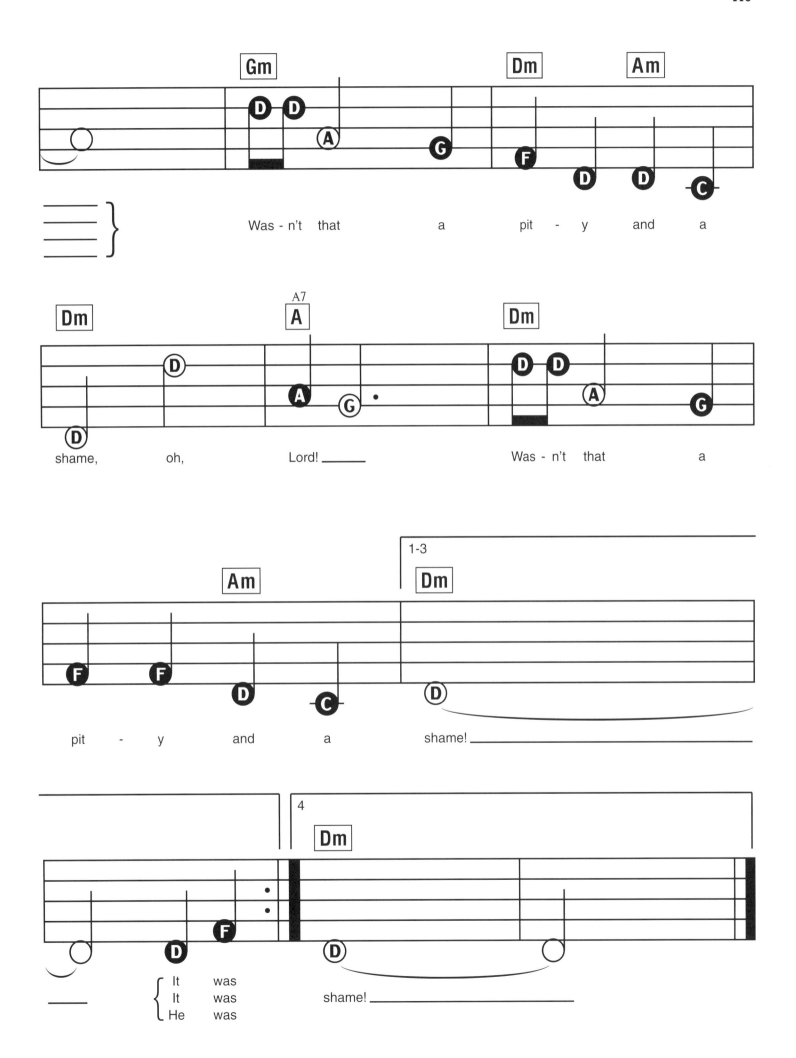

Santa Baby

Registration 3
Rhythm: Swing

By Joan Javits,
Phil Springer and Tony Springer

115

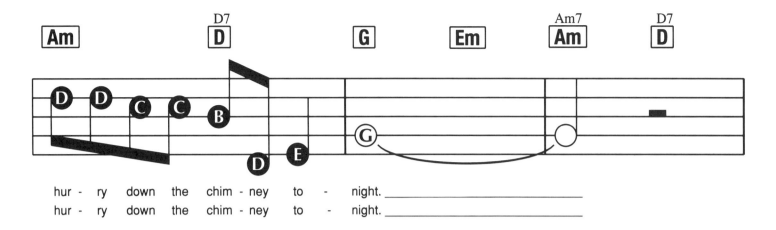

hur - ry down the chim - ney to - night. _____
hur - ry down the chim - ney to - night. _____

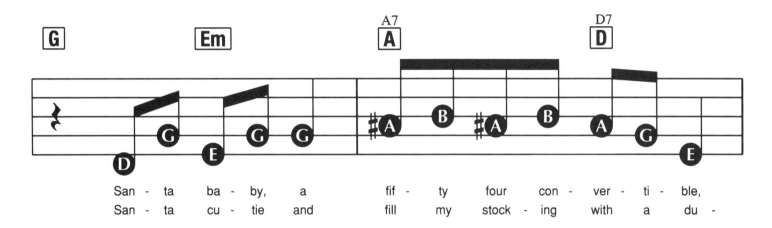

San - ta ba - by, a fif - ty four con - ver - ti - ble,
San - ta cu - tie and fill my stock - ing with a du -

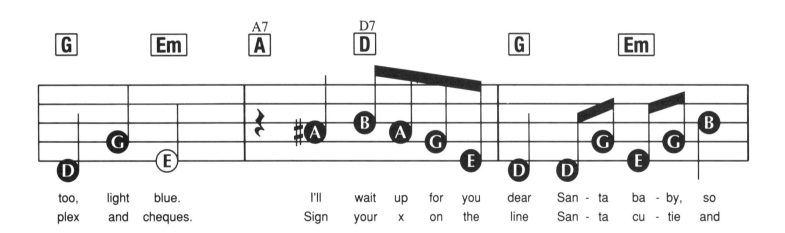

too, light blue. I'll wait up for you dear San - ta ba - by, so
plex and cheques. Sign your x on the line San - ta cu - tie and

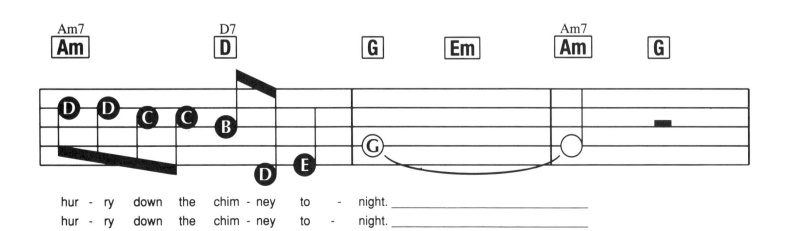

hur - ry down the chim - ney to - night. _____
hur - ry down the chim - ney to - night. _____

116

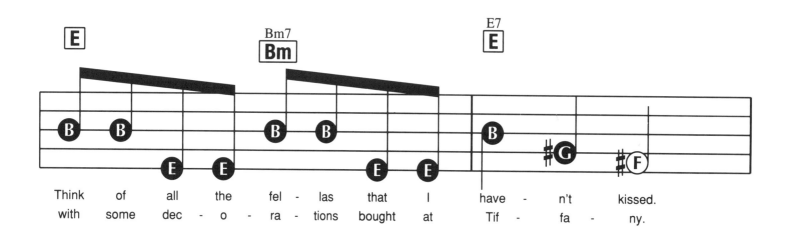

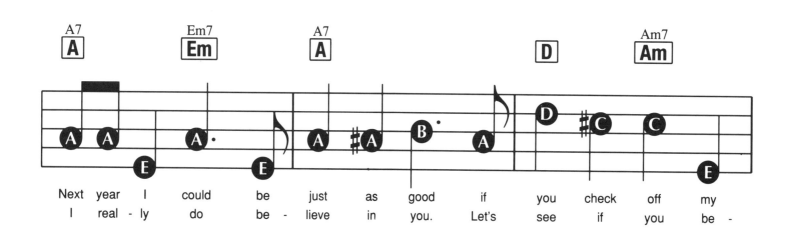

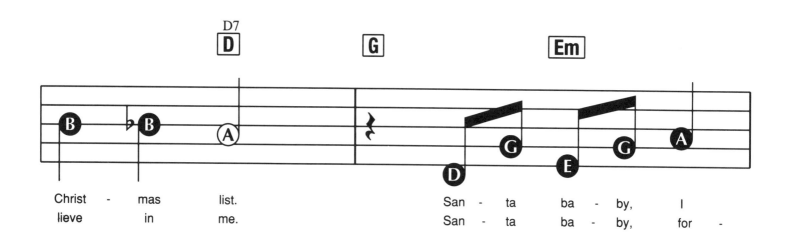

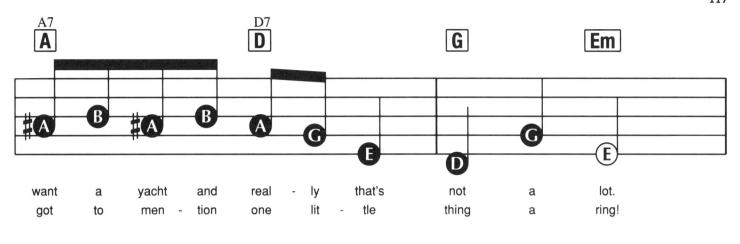

want   a   yacht   and   real - ly   that's   not   a   lot.
got   to   men - tion   one   lit - tle   thing   a   ring!

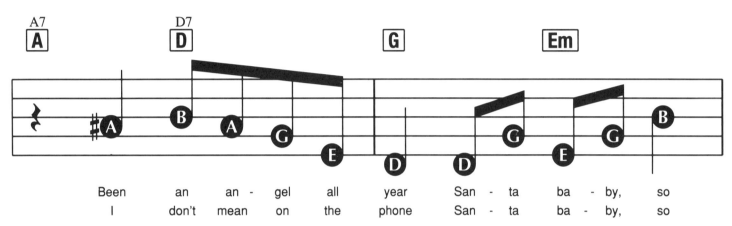

Been   an   an - gel   all   year   San - ta   ba - by,   so
I   don't   mean   on   the   phone   San - ta   ba - by,   so

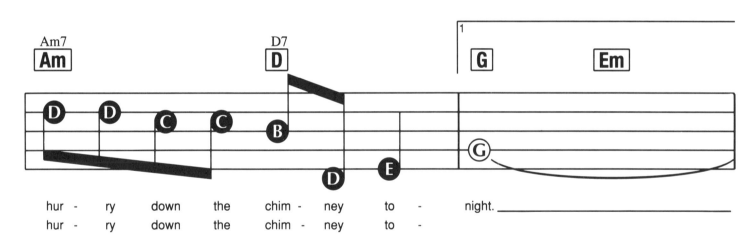

hur - ry   down   the   chim - ney   to -   night. _____
hur - ry   down   the   chim - ney   to -

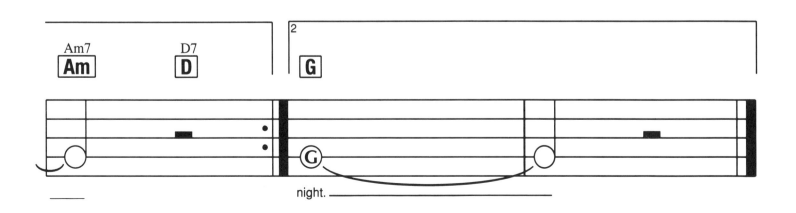

_____   night. _____

This Little Child

Registration 2
Rhythm: 4/4 Ballad or 8 Beat

Words and Music by
Scott Wesley Brown

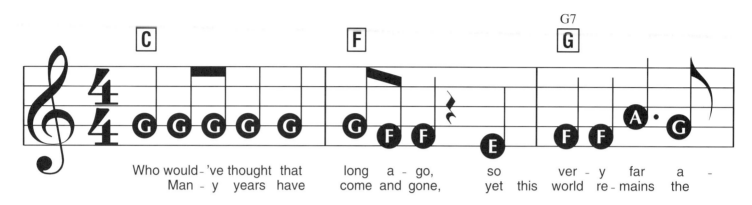

Who would-'ve thought that long a-go, so ver-y far a-
Man-y years have come and gone, yet this world re-mains the

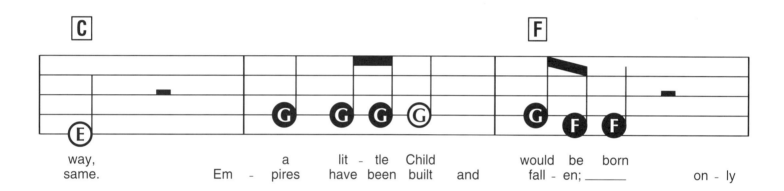

way, a lit-tle Child would be born
same. Em - pires have been built and fall-en; on-ly

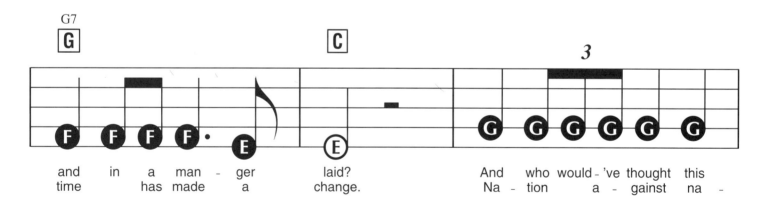

and in a man-ger laid? And who would-'ve thought this
time has made a change. Na-tion a-gainst na-

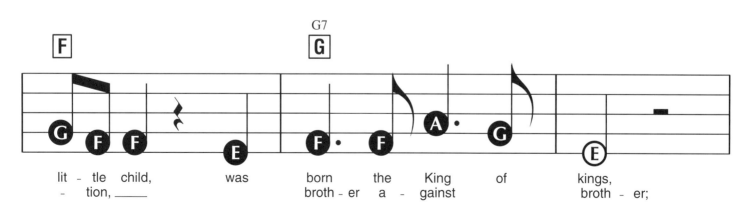

lit-tle child, was born the King of kings,
-tion, broth-er a-gainst broth-er;

119

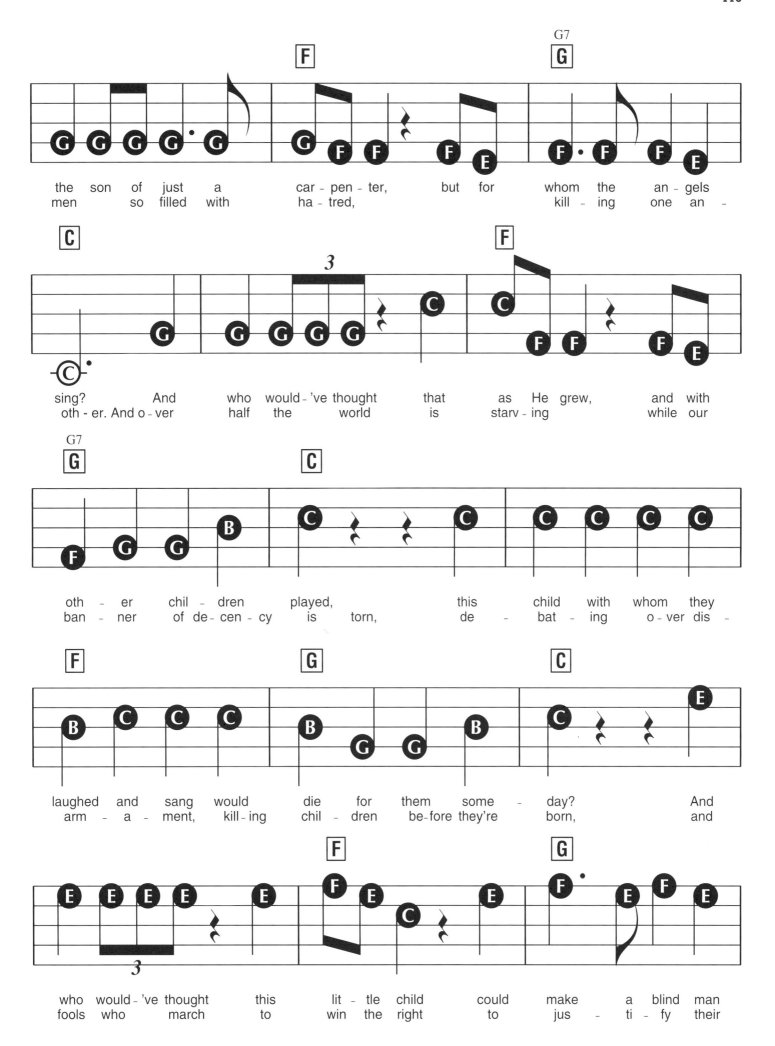

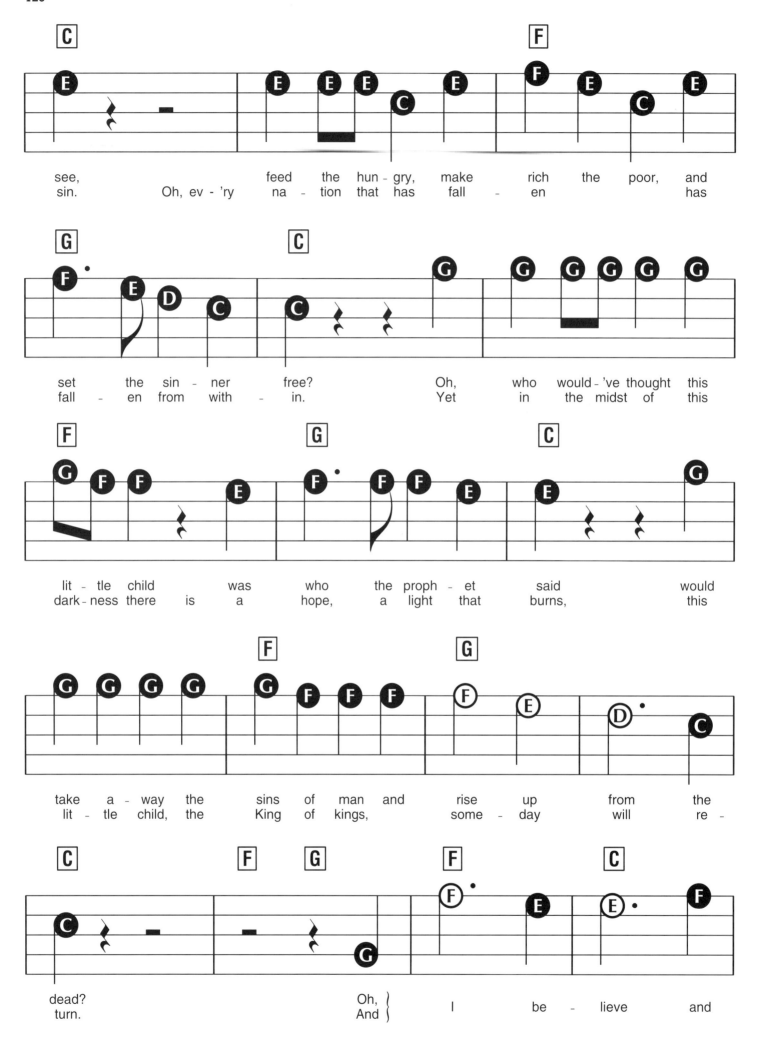

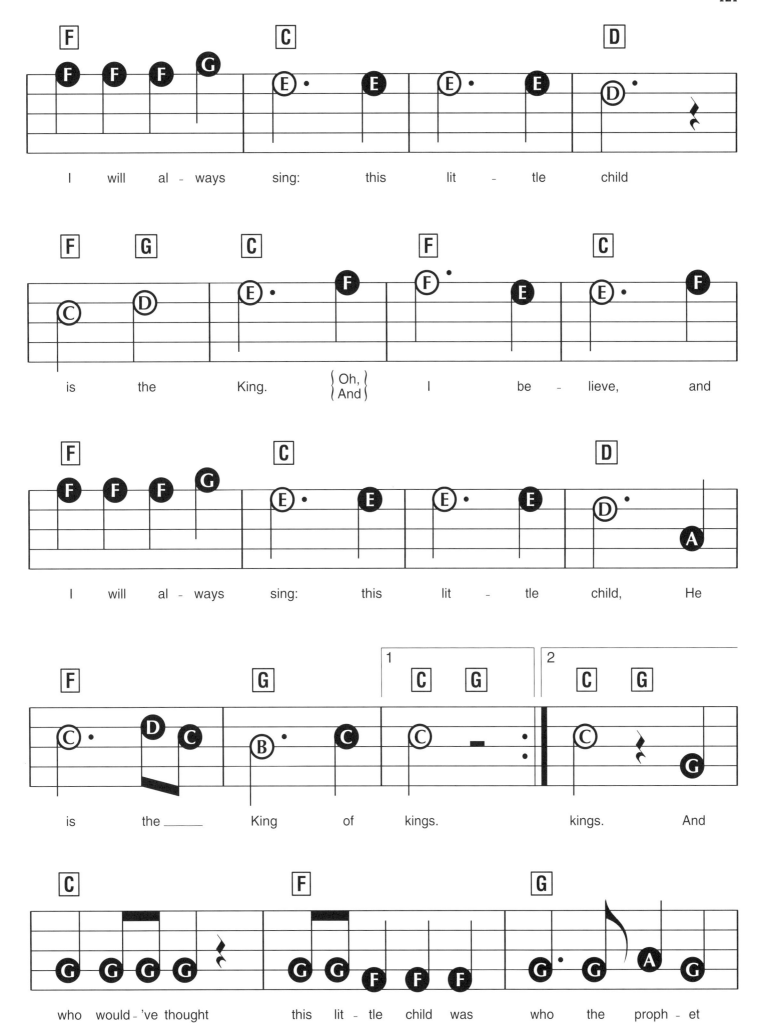

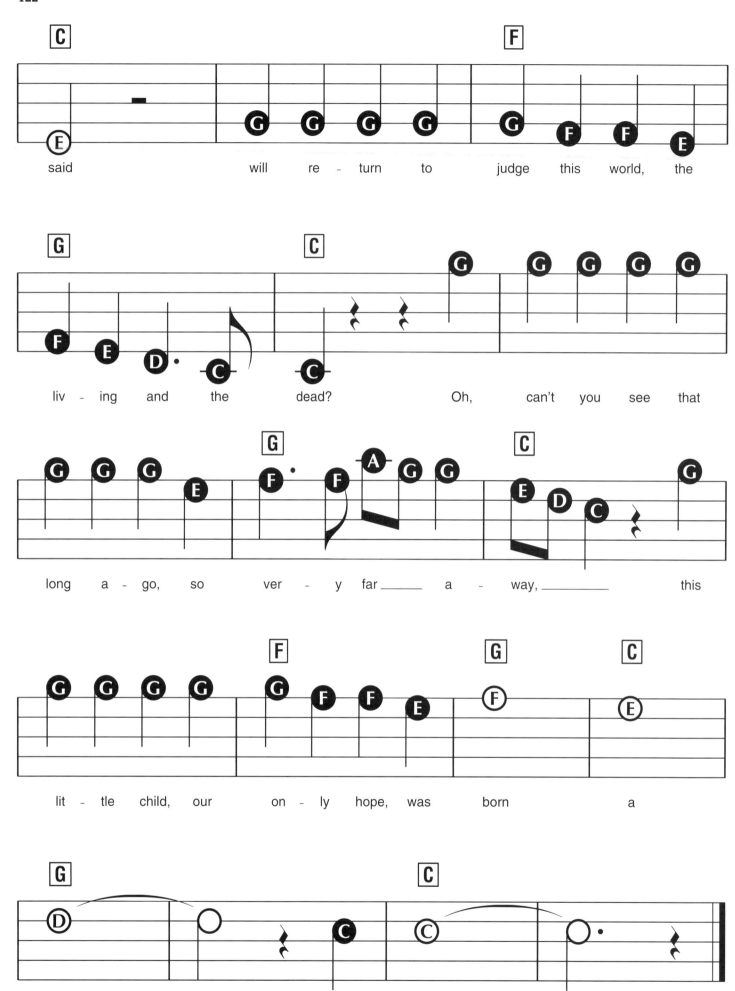

What a Merry Christmas This Could Be

Registration 8
Rhythm: Country or Fox Trot

Words and Music by Hank Cochran
and Harlan Howard

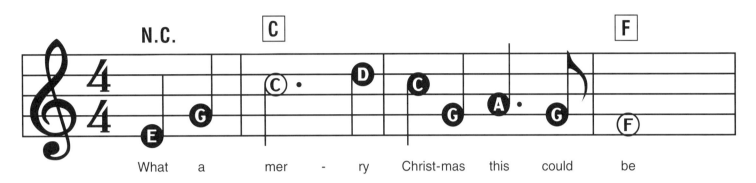

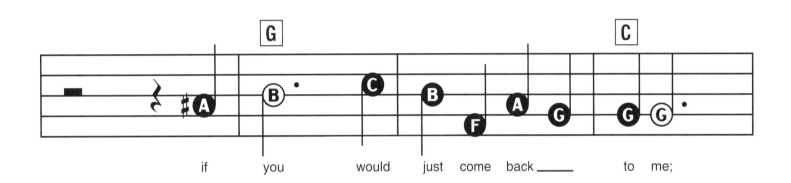

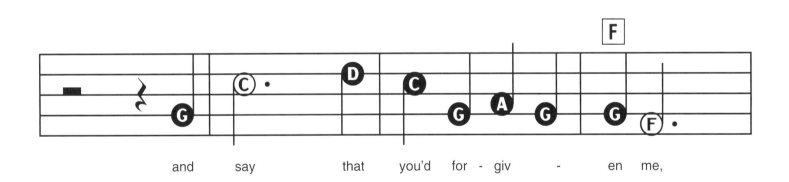

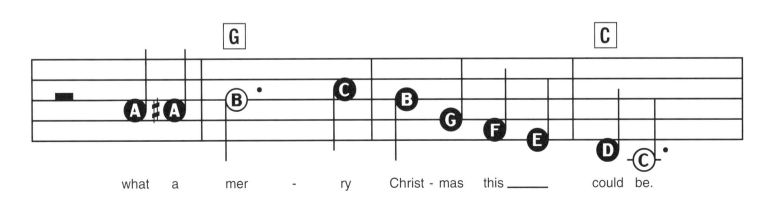

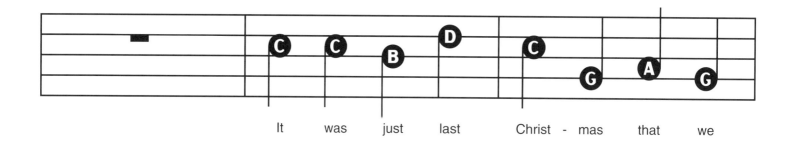

It was just last Christ-mas that we

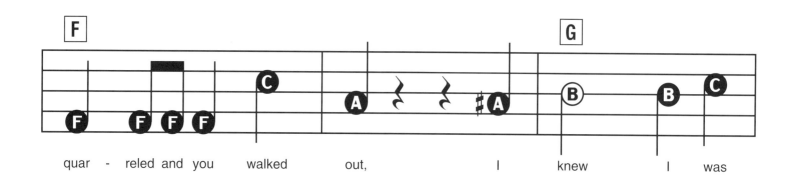

quar - reled and you walked out, I knew I was

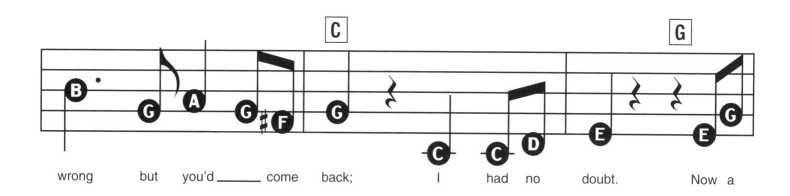

wrong but you'd _____ come back; I had no doubt. Now a

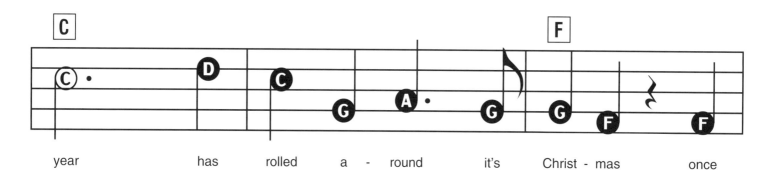

year has rolled a - round it's Christ-mas once

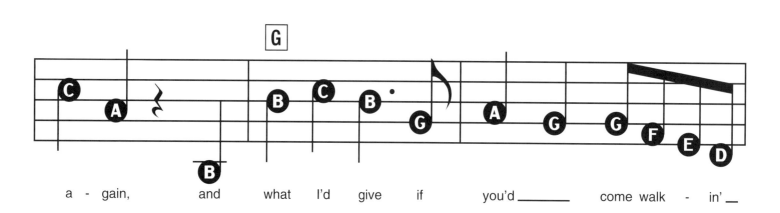

a - gain, and what I'd give if you'd _____ come walk - in' __

125

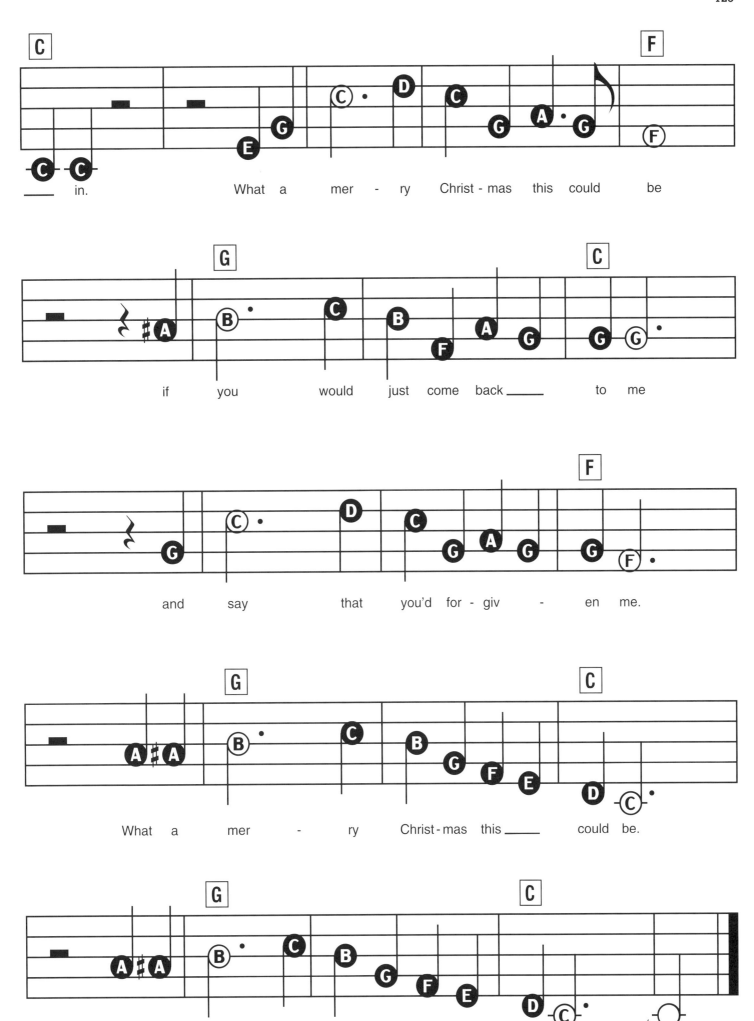

Where Are You Christmas?
from DR. SEUSS' HOW THE GRINCH STOLE CHRISTMAS

Registration 3
Rhythm: 4/4 Ballad

Words and Music by Will Jennings,
James Horner and Mariah Carey

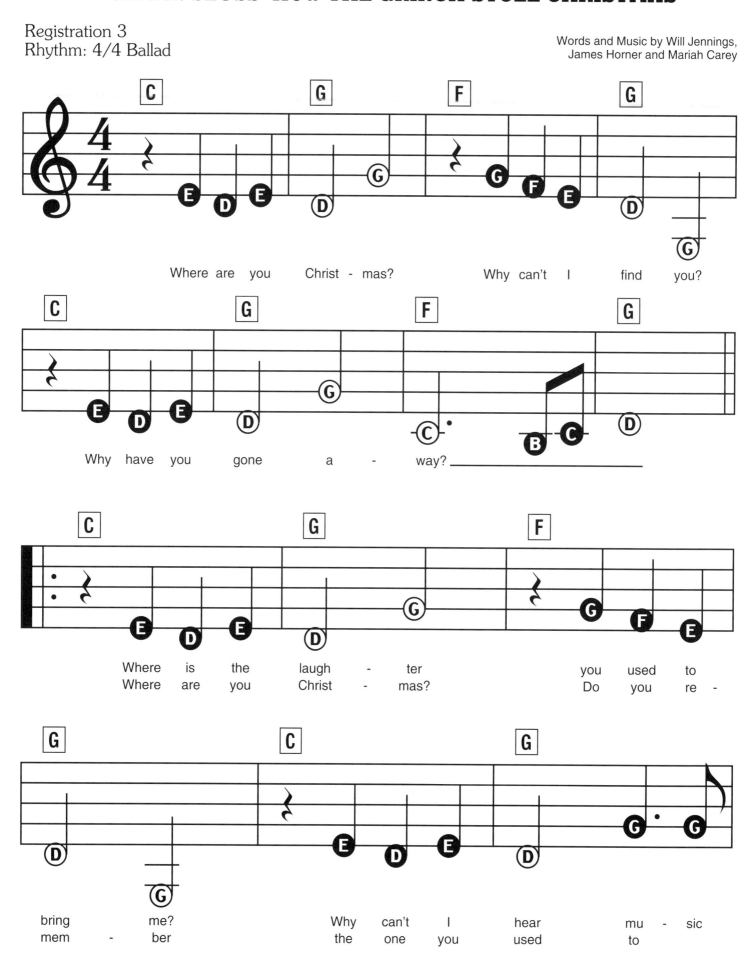

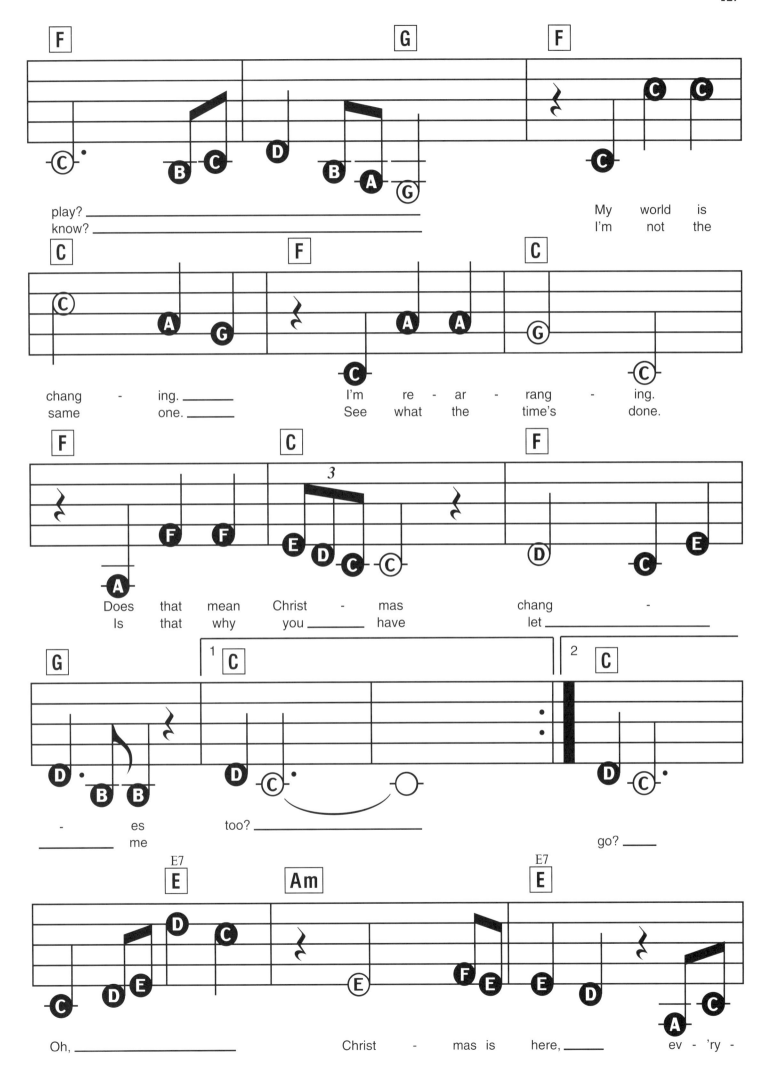

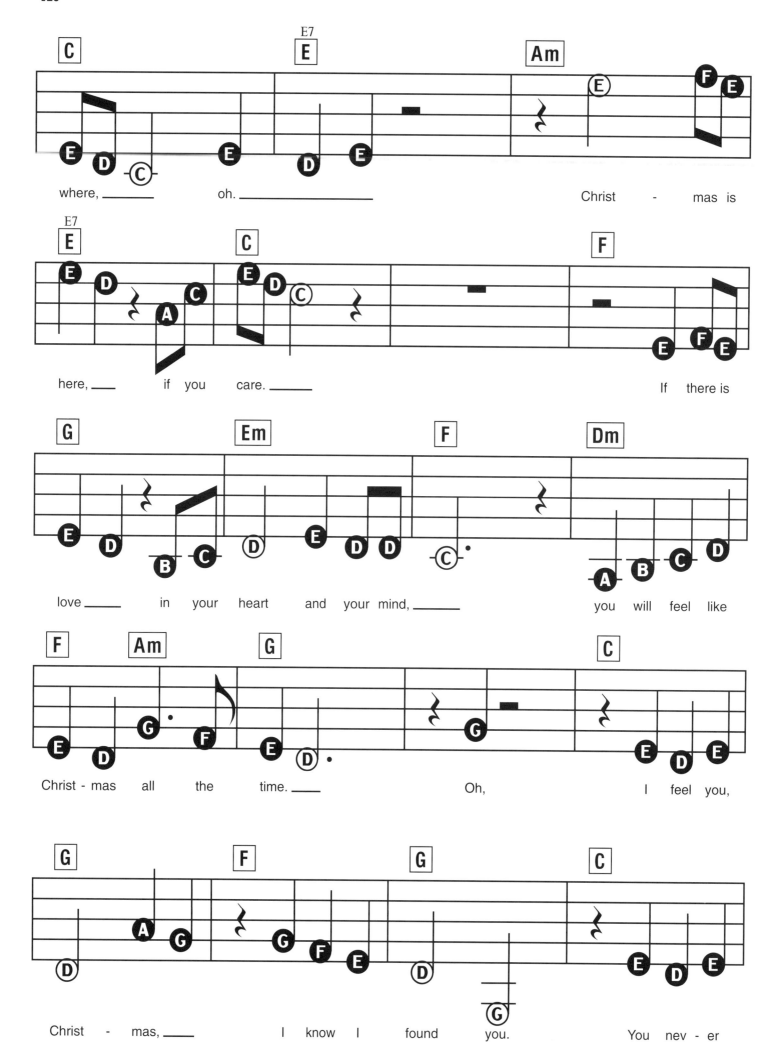

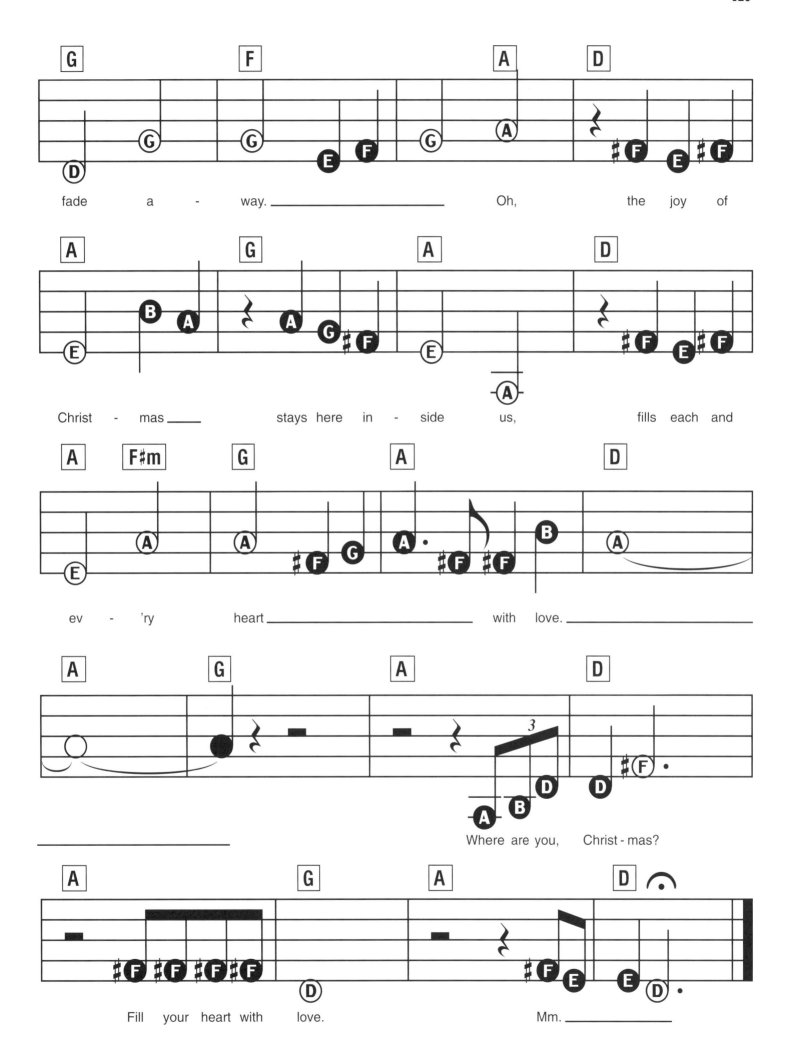

Why Christmas

Registration 8
Rhythm: R&B or Rock

Words and Music by
Wanya Morris

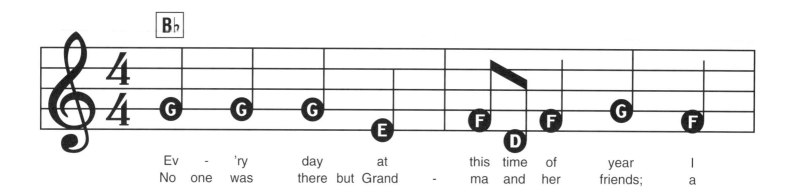

Ev - 'ry   day   at   this   time   of   year,   I
No   one   was   there   but   Grand - ma   and   her   friends;   a

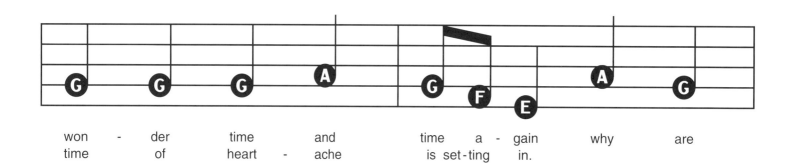

won - der   time   and   time   a - gain   why   are
time   of   time   heart - ache   is   set-ting   in.

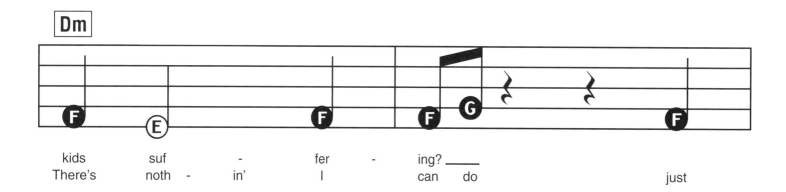

kids   suf   -   fer - ing? ____
There's   noth - in'   I   can   do   just

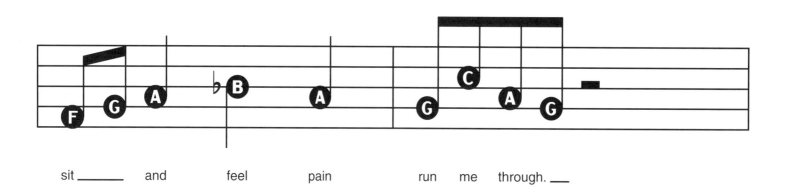

sit ____ and   feel   pain   run   me   through. ___

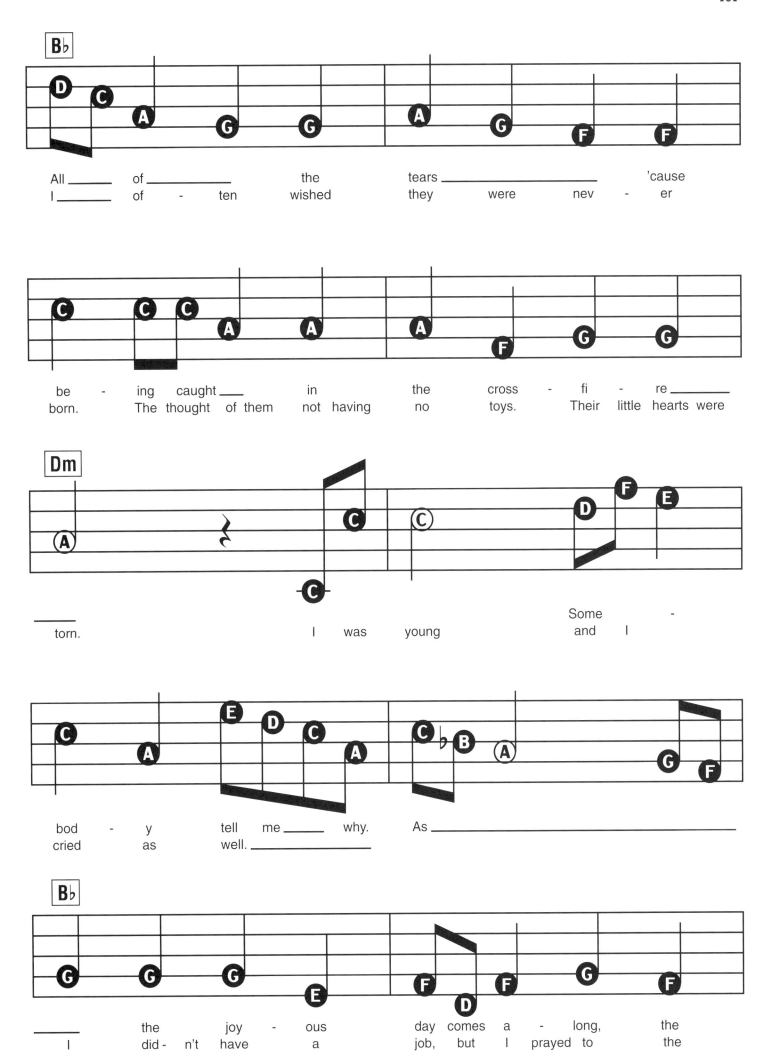

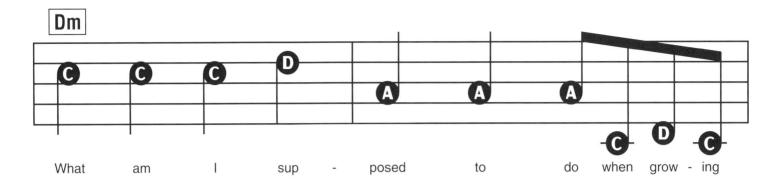

What am I sup - posed to do when grow - ing

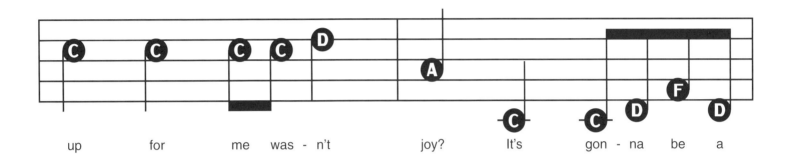

up for me was - n't joy? It's gon - na be a

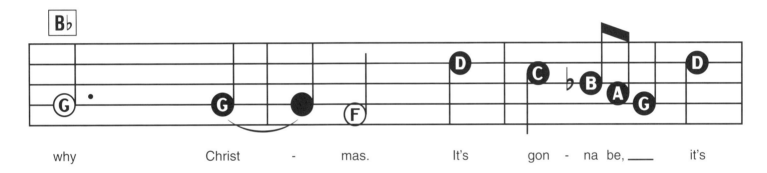

why Christ - mas. It's gon - na be,___ it's

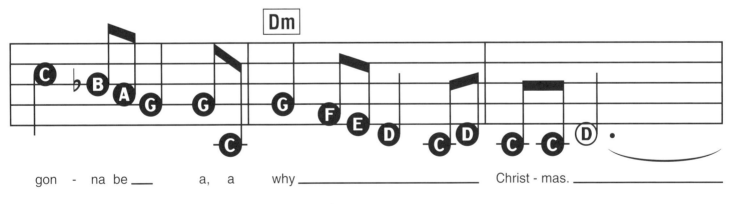

gon - na be ___ a, a why _____ Christ - mas. _____

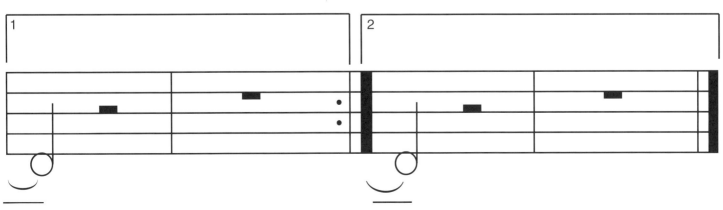

Who Would Imagine a King

from the Touchstone Motion Picture THE PREACHER'S WIFE

Registration 8
Rhythm: Waltz

Words and Music by Mervyn Warren
and Hallerin Hilton Hill

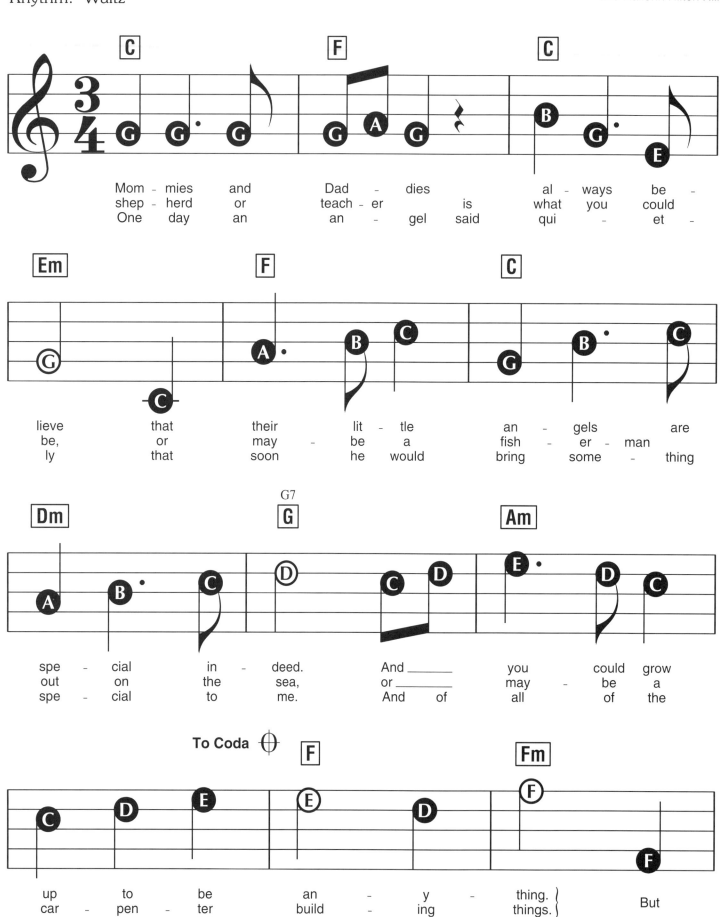

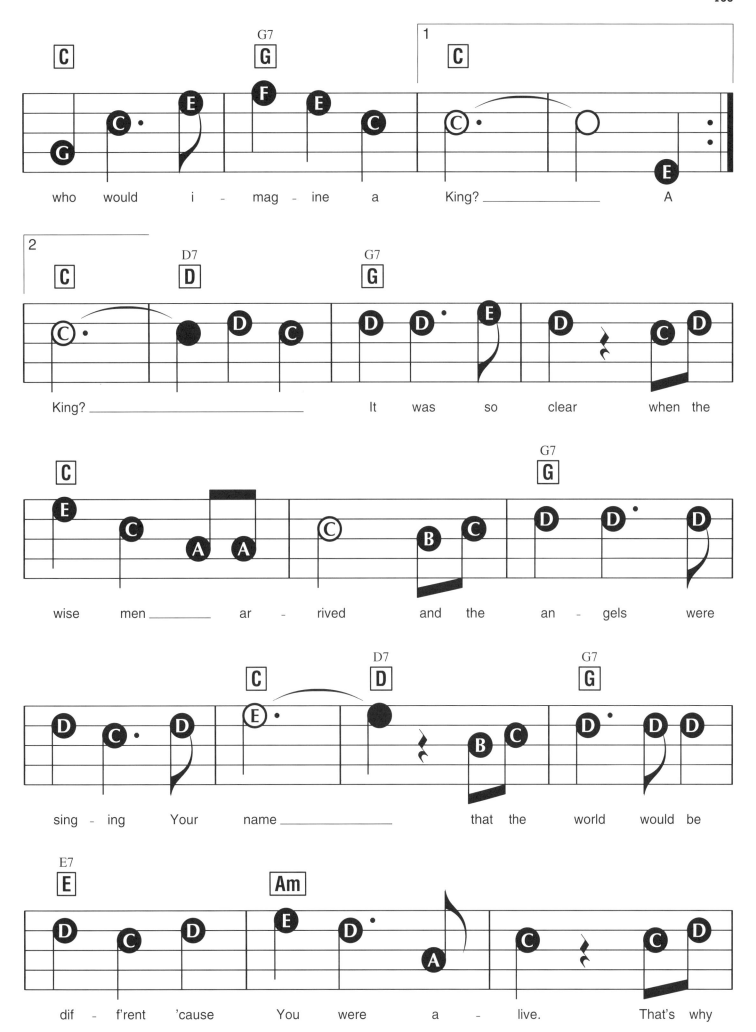

136

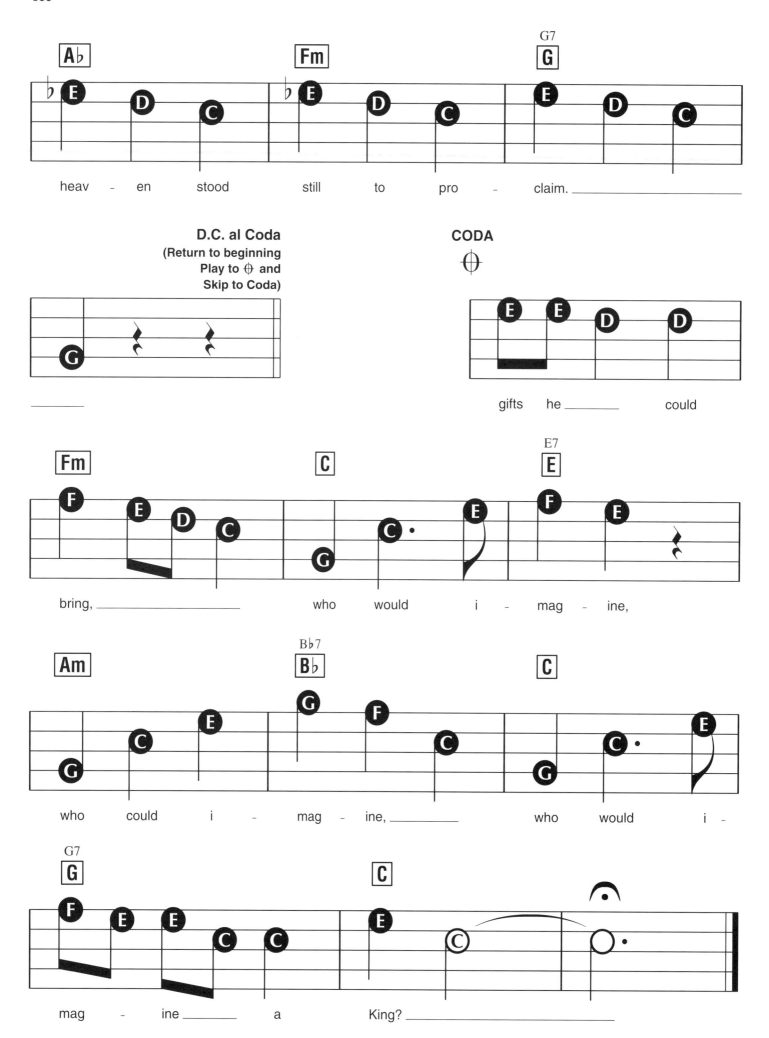